INSIGHT'S
BIBLE APPLICATION GUIDE
Joshua – Esther
A LIFE LESSON FROM EVERY CHAPTER

D0354014

From the Bible-Teaching Ministry of
CHARLES R. SWINDOLL

Insight's Bible Application Guide: Joshua–Esther
A Life Lesson from Every Chapter
From the Bible-Teaching Ministry of Charles R. Swindoll

Charles R. Swindoll has devoted his life to the accurate, practical teaching and application of God's Word and His grace. A pastor at heart, Chuck has served as senior pastor to congregations in Texas, Massachusetts, and California. Since 1998, he has served as the founder and senior pastor-teacher of Stonebriar Community Church in Frisco, Texas, but Chuck's listening audience extends far beyond a local church body. As a leading program in Christian broadcasting since 1979, *Insight for Living* airs in major Christian radio markets around the world, reaching people groups in languages they can understand. Chuck's extensive writing ministry has also served the body of Christ worldwide and his leadership as president and now chancellor of Dallas Theological Seminary has helped prepare and equip a new generation for ministry. Chuck and Cynthia, his partner in life and ministry, have four grown children, ten grandchildren, and two great-grandchildren.

Published By: IFL Publishing House, A Division of Insight for Living Ministries,
Post Office Box 251007, Plano, Texas 75025-1007

Editor in Chief: Cynthia Swindoll, President, Insight for Living
Executive Vice President: Wayne Stiles, Th.M., D.Min., Dallas Theological Seminary
Writers: Charles R. Swindoll, C.Th., Dallas Theological Seminary, D.D., L.H.D., LL.D., Litt.D.
    John Adair, Th.M., Ph.D., Dallas Theological Seminary
    Andrea Hitefield, M.A., Media and Communications, Dallas Theological Seminary
    Malia Rodriguez, Th.M., Dallas Theological Seminary
Content Editors: Kathryn Merritt, M.A., English, Hardin-Simmons University
    Amy L. Snedaker, B.A., English, Rhodes College
Copy Editors: Jim Craft, M.A., English, Mississippi College
    Paula McCoy, B.A., English, Texas A&M University-Commerce
Project Coordinators, Creative Ministries: Noelle Caple, M.A., Christian Education, Dallas Theological Seminary
    Megan Meckstroth, B.S., Advertising, University of Florida
Project Coordinator, Publishing: Melissa Cleghorn, B.A., University of North Texas
Proofreader: Paula McCoy, B.A., English, Texas A&M University-Commerce
Designer: Margaret Gulliford, B.A., Graphic Design, Taylor University
Production Artist: Nancy Gustine, B.F.A., Advertising Art, University of North Texas

ISBN: 978-1-57972-967-7
Printed in the United States of America

Table of Contents

A Letter from Chuck

One of the things that has always attracted me to the Bible is its intense practicality. Stories of failure and success, pain and victory, oppression and freedom flow through the pages of Scripture. Who doesn't know what it feels like to fail? Who hasn't relished the opportunity to overcome a heartrending, scandalous sin? The Bible's relevance to our everyday lives is as real and as current as it's ever been.

Is that true of the Old Testament as well? Absolutely! Who hasn't shaken in fear like Gideon before dealing with a critical problem? Many have struggled as David did, trying to stay faithful even though beset by repeated trials. What woman hasn't experienced the tension Esther felt between being treated as an object of fleshly desire and being seen as a respected and valued member of the household?

You will find these real-life situations and many others like them addressed in *Insight's Bible Application Guide: Joshua – Esther.* This second volume in the series takes you through every chapter of the Bible's Historical Books—even the lengthy genealogy that begins 1 Chronicles!—and shares practical advice on how to apply them. We have already released our initial volume on the first five books of the Bible . . . and future volumes will cover the Wisdom and Prophetic Books of the Old Testament, as well as the books of the New Testament. When completed, the *Insight's Bible Application Guide* series will guide you through every chapter of all sixty-six books of the Bible.

Believers in every era of history have sought to apply biblical insights and principles to their lives. But taking to heart the counsel of James 1:22 has proven more difficult than its simple wording suggests. Use this series to help you apply God's Word to your everyday life. Don't just hear the Word. Don't just read the Word. Do your best to *follow the Word*. Make it a reality from one day to the next.

Charles R. Swindoll

About the Writers

Charles R. Swindoll

Charles R. Swindoll has devoted his life to the accurate, practical teaching and application of God's Word and His grace. A pastor at heart, Chuck has served as senior pastor to congregations in Texas, Massachusetts, and California. Since 1998, he has served as the founder and senior pastor-teacher of Stonebriar Community Church in Frisco, Texas, but Chuck's listening audience extends far beyond a local church body. As a leading program in Christian broadcasting since 1979, *Insight for Living* airs in major Christian radio markets around the world, reaching people groups in languages they can understand. Chuck's extensive writing ministry has also served the body of Christ worldwide and his leadership as president and now chancellor of Dallas Theological Seminary has helped prepare and equip a new generation for ministry. Chuck and Cynthia, his partner in life and ministry, have four grown children, ten grandchildren, and two great-grandchildren. Chuck contributed the chapters on 1 Samuel, 2 Samuel, Nehemiah, and Esther.

John Adair

Th.M., Ph.D., Dallas Theological Seminary

John received his bachelor's degree from Criswell College and his master of theology degree from Dallas Theological Seminary, where he also completed his Ph.D. in Historical Theology. He serves as a writer in the Creative Ministries Department of

Insight for Living. John, his wife, Laura, and their three children reside in Frisco, Texas. John contributed the chapters on Judges, 2 Kings, and 1 Chronicles.

Andrea Hitefield

M.A., Media and Communication, Dallas Theological Seminary

Andrea holds a bachelor's degree from Moody Bible Institute and a master of arts degree in Media and Communication from Dallas Theological Seminary. While pursuing her master's degree, Andrea completed an internship at Insight for Living, where she was mentored by the writing and editing team. Andrea serves as the freshman grade director at Irving Bible Church and currently lives in Dallas, Texas. Andrea contributed the chapter on Ruth.

Malia Rodriguez

Th.M., Dallas Theological Seminary

Malia received her master of theology degree in Systematic Theology from Dallas Theological Seminary. She now serves as a writer in the Creative Ministries Department of Insight for Living, where she is able to merge her love of theology with her gift for words. Malia and her husband, Matt, who is also a graduate of Dallas Theological Seminary, live in the Dallas area with their son. Malia contributed the chapters on Joshua, 1 Kings, 2 Chronicles, and Ezra.

What Is the Value of the Historical Books Today?

We all have been shaped by the past. Memories both painful and joyful line the halls of our minds, influencing and transforming us. In many cases, events that took place before we were even born can have effects that continue into the present. History records significant events and notable people for the benefit of those who follow. The Historical Books of the Old Testament offer a record of Israel's history. And though these events took place long ago in a place far from most of us, the memories contained within have the potential for deep spiritual impact in the lives of God's people.

First, reading the history of God's people allows us to learn from and avoid their past mistakes as well as emulate heroic deeds of old. When Saul faltered due to his self-sufficient and impatient pride, we understand the need for self-control and dependence on others (1 Samuel 15:1–29). On the other hand, Jonathan's friendship with David was characterized by commitment and integrity, two qualities to which the people of today should also aspire (1 Samuel 18:1–4).

Second, history shows us the often baffling complexity of human beings in a specific and relatable context, faithfully serving God one moment, only to fail Him miserably the next. We soar with Gideon as he initially destroys the idols of Baal and leads his people in battle (Judges 6:25–27; 7:19–21). And yet, Gideon's biblical story ends with his leading his people into another form of idolatry (8:27). Complex histories like Gideon's remind us to treat others with grace and patience by drawing our attention to practical actions rather than noodling on abstract doctrine.

Finally, those who take the time to work through the books of Joshua – Esther can draw from the stories a keener understanding of our God. When Nehemiah heard that his people — God's people — were distressed back in the Promised Land, he asked God to allow him to return to the land and help the people rebuild (Nehemiah 2:4 – 5). God had not forgotten His people. He heard Nehemiah and, through the word of King Artaxerxes, allowed Nehemiah to go back to Jerusalem and help his people. God's attributes do not change. Nehemiah could rely on God's faithfulness and compassion in ancient times, and we still can today.

History matters. If we have ears to hear and eyes to see, history can teach us what it means to be truly human in this world, to serve God well, and to live in a way that brings Him glory. May God kindle our hearts for these valuable lessons through our reading the ancient memories of and about His people.

INSIGHT'S
BIBLE APPLICATION GUIDE
Joshua – Esther

Joshua

Joshua 1

"Just as I have been with Moses, I will be with you; I will not fail you or forsake you. Be strong and courageous, for you shall give this people possession of the land which I swore to their fathers to give them. Only be strong and very courageous." —Joshua 1:5–7

Forty years earlier, Joshua had stood with Caleb and Moses and urged the Israelites to face fortified cities and intimidating opponents. But now, Moses was dead. Joshua would have to lead the people alone. As Joshua gazed westward toward the hills that led up into the will of God, the Lord graciously reminded His servant: "I will not fail you." Therefore, Joshua could "be strong and courageous." As with Joshua, God's will for us often seems uphill, mysterious, lonely—and frightening. The Lord leads us places that force us to trust Him. We need more than physical strength to face challenges; we need strength of character that comes from meditating on and applying the Bible (2 Timothy 3:16–17). Only then can we proceed confidently in the will of God (Joshua 1:8; Romans 12:2). Then we can be strong and courageous, knowing that God will never fail us or forsake us (Matthew 28:20).

Joshua 2

"When we heard it, our hearts melted and no courage remained in any man any longer because of you; for the LORD your God, He is God in heaven above and on earth beneath." —Joshua 2:11

Joshua dispatched two spies to survey the land, including Jericho. Providence led them to the house of a harlot named Rahab. When Jericho's king discovered the spies' whereabouts, Rahab lied and sent the king's men in the wrong direction. Later, as she spoke with the spies, she revealed that all the Canaanites were terrified because they had heard how God had parted the Red Sea and recently defeated the Amorites. Rahab then declared her belief in the God of Israel and requested her household might escape Jericho's inevitable destruction. Her words affirm timeless truths. Any nation God has ultimately destroyed had first received at least some revelation to accept or to reject (Genesis 15:16; Jeremiah 18:7–10; Romans 1:20). Any individual whom God converts comes to Him based on faith—not on the morality of the one believing (Titus 3:5; Hebrews 11:31). Rahab's significant descendants reveal God's readiness to use any of us for His glory (Matthew 1:5).

Joshua 3

Then Joshua said to the people, "Consecrate yourselves, for tomorrow the Lord will do wonders among you." . . . *So the people crossed [the Jordan River] opposite Jericho.*   *—Joshua 3:5, 16*

Only one obstacle stood between the Hebrews and Jericho—the Jordan River. Joshua's command to "consecrate yourselves" refers to keeping oneself pure from unclean things. For Joshua, personal purity reflected a belief that this whole business of crossing the Jordan and taking the Promised Land would occur as a holy act of God. For starters, wandering in the wilderness for forty years didn't afford the Hebrews many opportunities to learn to swim. The river raged at flood stage as Joshua and the nation prepared to cross. In our lives, most of the obstacles we encounter appear to be merely physical. A river. A relationship. A salary. A disease.

But the greater barrier God wants to ford is the one in our hearts, which our physical obstacles serve to reveal (Ephesians 6:2). This is the crossing from fear to faith. Only God can part the waters.

Joshua 4

"The LORD your God dried up the waters of the Jordan before you until you had crossed, just as the LORD your God had done to the Red Sea, which He dried up before us until we had crossed."

—Joshua 4:23

Joshua compared the parting of the Jordan with the parting of the Red Sea. He linked the power of God that redeemed the people from slavery in Egypt to the power that allowed them to enter Canaan. In other words, the same grace that redeemed them would carry them into their new land. Our deliverance as Christians from bondage to sin and our entrance into God's rest both stem from the same act of grace at the cross. In fact, the author of Hebrews compares Joshua's entering Canaan with our entering the rest God provides those who believe in Christ apart from works (Hebrews 4:1–10). Perhaps this is why hymn writers often use crossing the Jordan River as a metaphor for entering heaven. What Joshua pointed out to Israel is a truth we should also embrace: the grace that saved us to begin with is the grace that will lead us home (Philippians 1:6).[1]

Joshua 5

The captain of the Lord's host said to Joshua, "Remove your sandals from your feet, for the place where you are standing is holy." And Joshua did so.   *—Joshua 5:15*

Joshua had just witnessed God's miraculous parting of the Jordan River as the Hebrews walked through it into the Promised Land. Overwhelmed by the Lord's provision and faithfulness, Joshua took a walk to reflect on what God had done. As Joshua walked, he encountered an angelic soldier. When the soldier told Joshua to take off his sandals because the ground he stood on was holy, Joshua surely remembered the story Moses had told him about the burning bush, sandals, and holy ground (Exodus 3:5). And just as God had commissioned Moses to lead His people out of Egypt, He appointed Joshua to lead the Israelites in a miraculous victory over Jericho. For Christians, all ground is holy ground. We don't have to wait for a secret message or a phenomenal encounter. The Lord speaks to us today through the Bible, and He expects us to treat its words and our lives as holy.

Joshua 6

Then Joshua made them take an oath at that time, saying, "Cursed before the Lord is the man who rises up and builds this city Jericho; with the loss of his firstborn he shall lay its foundation, and with the loss of his youngest son he shall set up its gates."   *—Joshua 6:26*

God intended the ruins of Jericho to be a perpetual, smoldering heap of memories for the Israelites. The defeat of Jericho marked the beginning of the Israelites' conquest of Canaan. When they leveled this strategic city, news spread and instilled fear in the other inhabitants of the Promised Land. And because of Jericho's central location, God's people would inevitably pass by the ruins of the city and remember His power, provision, and promises. The Lord still works in amazing ways. When believers pray for friends and family members, God works mightily in their lives. And when we have a financial, relational, or emotional need, God often meets that need in inexplicable ways. As Christians, what events in our lives point us back to God's power, provision, and promises? Let's develop creative ways to remember the "Jerichos" in our lives — the strategic, faith-building deeds of God.

Joshua 7

So the LORD said to Joshua, "Rise up! Why is it that you have fallen on your face? Israel has sinned. . . . And they have even taken some of the things under the ban and have both stolen and deceived. Moreover, they have also put them among their own things."
—Joshua 7:10–11

After Joshua had spied out the land of Ai, he sent three thousand troops to attack its people. But the army of Ai prevailed and all the Israelites shuddered in fear. So Joshua asked God why He parted the Jordan River and led them into Canaan. Hadn't the Lord promised to defeat the inhabitants of the Promised Land? When God didn't seem to come through, Joshua doubted. But something had happened that Joshua didn't know about. Sin had infiltrated the camps of Israel. After the defeat of Jericho, Achan kept some of the spoils for himself, even though all the gold and silver belonged to God. When hidden sin lies under the surface of our lives, it's no wonder we experience defeat. As Christians, we should regularly take inventory of our hearts, confess any hidden sin to the Lord, and trust that He will extend grace as we face the consequences.

Joshua 8

There was not a word of all that Moses had commanded which Joshua did not read before all the assembly of Israel with the women and the little ones and the strangers who were living among them.
—Joshua 8:35

After Joshua dealt with Achan's sin, the Lord gave the people victory over Ai. And this time, all of the Israelites followed God's commandments. The Lord had told His people to kill all of the citizens of Ai but to keep the cattle and the spoil for themselves. The Lord had severely punished Achan for his sin at Jericho, so the people feared God. And because they feared the Lord, the Israelites obeyed Him. Joshua took this opportunity, when the people's hearts were tender toward God, to hold a rededication ceremony. Joshua built an altar, offered peace offerings, and reminded the Israelites to trust the Lord and obey His Word. Even though God extends grace, He doesn't remove sin's consequences. Christians should remember that God disciplines His children out of love so that our hearts will become soft, teachable, and pliable. Only then can the Lord reshape our stubborn wills so that they match His.

Joshua 9

So the men of Israel took some of their provisions, and did not ask for the counsel of the LORD. — *Joshua 9:14*

Joshua got duped. The crafty inhabitants of Gibeon knew they were next on Joshua's hit list, so they devised a plan to trick him into making a covenant with them. The Gibeonites pretended to live in a faraway land and to have come because they heard about God's victory over the Amorites. They wore tattered clothes, packed stale bread, and met Joshua on the road. Rather than taking time to pray for wisdom, Joshua believed their act and made a covenant with them. But when the Israelites got to Gibeon, they realized that they had made a pact with the enemy. Our culture provides many opportunities to make bad choices. When Christians make rash decisions about finances or relationships, and fail to seek God's guidance, we will have to deal with the consequences. But when we pray, read His Word, and wait for the Lord's response, He will give us wisdom to follow His will.

Joshua 10

Joshua captured all these kings and their lands at one time, because the LORD, the God of Israel, fought for Israel. — *Joshua 10:42*

One by one, Joshua and the Israelites marched through the cities of the Amorites and defeated them all. But they didn't do it on their own. God performed miracles on behalf of His people. The Lord confused the Amorites and made them vulnerable (Joshua 10:10), He rained down huge hailstones on them (10:11), He stopped the sun in its course for an entire day

(10:12–14), and He cornered the five kings of the Amorites in a cave so Joshua could finish them off (10:16). God had promised to fight on behalf of His people and He came through in unforgettable ways. God may not respond to believers' prayers today by stopping the sun or by punishing our rivals with natural disasters. But the Lord does help us fight our battles. God works in amazing ways through the indwelling Holy Spirit, who gives us strength to resist sin and obey God.

Joshua 11

Joshua did to them as the Lord had told him; he hamstrung their
horses and burned their chariots with fire.   —*Joshua 11:9*

Joshua was a great leader. He rallied the troops, he acted with courage, and he inspired loyalty in his followers. Joshua had received his leadership training from Moses, God's friend, the man who had seen the Lord face-to-face. But the most important quality that made Joshua a great leader was his obedience to God. When the Lord said He would defeat Israel's enemies, Joshua believed God and acted on faith. Even when an alliance of kings readied their armies to attack the Israelites, Joshua trusted God when He said, "Do not be afraid because of them, for tomorrow at this time I will deliver all of them slain before Israel" (Joshua 11:6). Spiritual leadership doesn't depend on charisma, experience, intelligence, or education. Godly leaders are those who love the Lord, know His Word inside and out, and walk in obedience by faith, believing that what God has said is actually true.

Joshua 12

Now these are the kings of the land whom Joshua and the sons of Israel defeated beyond the Jordan toward the west . . . and Joshua gave it to the tribes of Israel as a possession according to their divisions.
—Joshua 12:7

Joshua and the Israelite army had conquered the kingdoms of thirty-three kings. After all the difficult battles, the people must have looked back in awe at how God had fought for them. Joshua divided the land among the tribes of Israel and gave it to them as their inheritance. And as long as the people obeyed the Lord and followed His Law, He promised to bless them and establish them in the land. Finally, they had rest from their enemies, so they planned to enjoy the land God had given them. When God gives Christians victory over anger, jealousy, or other sins, we should keep track of the Lord's powerful work on our behalf. God promises to provide a way out when sin lures us (1 Corinthians 10:13). We can choose to follow Him. Then, when new temptations arise, believers can look back at God's perfect record of faithfulness and continue to trust Him.

Joshua 13

Now Joshua was old and advanced in years when the Lord said to him, "You are old and advanced in years, and very much of the land remains to be possessed."
—Joshua 13:1

Joshua didn't retire from serving God. He didn't cash in his 401k and begin living a life of leisure. Even as an elderly man, Joshua considered himself useful to the Lord. There was still a lot of land yet to be possessed, and the Lord planned to work through

Joshua to continue to divide it among the tribes of Israel. After many years of leading the Israelites, Joshua had gained wisdom that could benefit God's people. When Christians reach retirement age, we shouldn't stop serving God. Our culture values youth, energy, and vigor. But God values wisdom, experience, and long-term faithfulness. The Holy Spirit will use anyone who submits to Him, whether young or old. So as believers in Christ, let's not view retirement as a chance to spend our days in perpetual leisure. Let's use that time as an opportunity to serve God and others with more skill and vigor.

Joshua 14

"Nevertheless my brethren who went up with me made the heart of the people melt with fear; but I followed the LORD my God fully."
—*Joshua 14:8*

The time had finally come! Many years earlier, God had promised to reward Caleb for his faith, and it was time to claim his inheritance. Moses had sent twelve men, one from each tribe, to survey the land so they could make arrangements to take it over (Numbers 13). Caleb, a gutsy leader, represented the tribe of Judah. Ten of the spies discouraged the Israelites from marching into the Promised Land; only Caleb and Joshua urged the people to step out in faith, believing in God's promise to give them Canaan despite the obstacles. Caleb serves as an example of an encourager. An encourager is a person who knows God's promises, believes that He is faithful, and inspires others with the courage to trust the Lord. As Christians who have received forgiveness and eternal fellowship with God through Jesus Christ, we should be the most encouraging people around!

Joshua 15

Now as for the Jebusites, the inhabitants of Jerusalem, the sons of Judah could not drive them out; so the Jebusites live with the sons of Judah at Jerusalem until this day.   —*Joshua 15:63*

Jerusalem, the future capital of the southern kingdom of Judah and home of God's temple, had some pretty tough citizens. Though the Israelite warriors fought hard, they couldn't dislodge the Jebusites. Since God powerfully fought for His people and sovereignly helped them defeat the inhabitants of Canaan, why couldn't the Israelites drive out the Jebusites? Were the inhabitants of Jerusalem too strong for the Lord? Of course not! But the battles that the Israelites faced were often won or lost, based not on God's ability but on His people's faith. Sometimes the Israelites fought in their own strength without trusting God to defeat their enemies. Sometimes Christians face tough challenges and choose to trust in our own strength alone. And when we forget to rely on the Lord to help us, sometimes He lets us fail. Often it takes defeat to remind believers of our complete dependence on God.

Joshua 16

The sons of Joseph, Manasseh and Ephraim, received their inheritance.   —*Joshua 16:4*

When Jacob's sons sold his favorite son, Joseph, into slavery, Jacob thought Joseph was dead. But he was wrong. God redeemed the life of Joseph and used him to provide for Jacob and his family. And after many years, Jacob not only got to see Joseph, but he met Joseph's two sons, Manasseh and Ephraim. Elated, Jacob thanked the Lord and blessed each of Joseph's sons with a future inheritance in the Promised Land. Back in Genesis 48, Jacob blessed Joseph with a double portion, and in Joshua 16, Joshua honored Jacob's blessing by allotting two territories to Joseph's sons, one to Manasseh and one to Ephraim. This double portion of blessing reflects God's generosity toward His people. Though we deserve nothing, through faith in Christ, the Lord gives us everything—favor, unconditional love, fellowship with Him and others, material and spiritual provision, and the promise of resurrection.

Joshua 17

They came near before Eleazar the priest and before Joshua the son of Nun . . . saying, "The Lord commanded Moses to give us an inheritance among our brothers." So according to the command of the Lord he gave them an inheritance among their father's brothers.

—Joshua 17:4

Most people haven't heard of Mahlah, Noah, Hoglah, Milcah, and Tirzah. But these women played a significant role in the division of the Promised Land among God's people. Manasseh's descendant, Zelophehad, didn't have any sons. So his daughters spoke up and asked for their inheritance. Zelophehad had obeyed the Lord, and his daughters argued that even though he didn't have any sons, his name shouldn't be removed from the list of recipients (Numbers 27:1–11). These daughters trusted that the Lord would lead them into the Promised Land, and when they got there, they asked Joshua and Eleazar for their inheritance. God's grace and His promises extend equally to men and women. In Jesus Christ, both men and women have value, worth, and significance in God's plan (Galatians 3:27–29). God doesn't show favoritism, so neither should we. Let's examine our hearts and confess our prejudices to the Lord.

Joshua 18

*So Joshua said to the sons of Israel, "How long will you put off enter-
ing to take possession of the land which the LORD, the God of your
fathers, has given you?"* —*Joshua 18:3*

The Lord despises selfishness. God had promised to give the
Israelites the land of Canaan. But when Moses had sent twelve
spies to check out the land, ten tribal leaders had refused to fight.
Their selfishness prevented them from claiming God's promise.
And years later, after God had given them many victories, seven
of these same tribes still refused to fight for their inheritance.
Therefore, Joshua commanded the tribes of Benjamin, Simeon,
Zebulun, Issachar, Asher, Naphtali, and Dan to pick three men
from each tribe to survey the rest of the land so Joshua could
cast lots and divide it equally. How often do we Christians drag
our feet when it comes to obeying God? If we're more concerned
with meeting our own needs than following God's Word, we will
likely miss the blessing that comes from obedience. Let's value
the Lord's commands above our own desires.

Joshua 19

*Then the second lot fell to Simeon, to the tribe of the sons of Simeon
according to their families, and their inheritance was in the midst of
the inheritance of the sons of Judah.* —*Joshua 19:1*

Simeon was a violent man set on revenge. After Shechem the
Hivite raped Simeon's sister, Dinah, and then asked for her
hand in marriage, Simeon and his brothers tricked the men of
Shechem's house into getting circumcised. Then, when they were
weak from the procedure, Simeon and Levi killed them all as

punishment for Dinah's rape (Genesis 34). The brothers took revenge into their own hands instead of trusting God to judge. Therefore, Jacob promised to scatter Simeon's descendants in the Promised Land (49:7). When Joshua drew their lot, they received various scattered cities in Judah. Simeon had taken retribution into his own hands, and his descendants suffered the consequences. Likewise, when Christians today take vengeance into our own hands, God will hold us accountable. Only the Lord can exact punishment with impartiality and perfect justice. So, when Christians or non-Christians sin, we must entrust them into God's just and gracious hands (Romans 12:19).

Joshua 20

Then the LORD spoke to Joshua, saying, "Speak to the sons of Israel, saying, 'Designate the cities of refuge, of which I spoke to you through Moses.'"
—Joshua 20:1–2

After he divided the land among the tribes of Israel, Joshua reminded the people to set up the cities of refuge, as Moses had commanded them in Deuteronomy 19. These cities provided refuge to members of God's people who unintentionally killed a fellow Israelite, so that a relative of the deceased person wouldn't avenge the death by murdering the unintentional killer. Once the manslayer entered one of the cities of refuge, the elders were obligated to protect him. So what can Christians learn from God's provision of cities of refuge? We should remember that God provides refuge for His people. And when we sin, we should run toward the Lord, not away from Him. Through Christ, we have received forgiveness. "As far as the east is from

the west, / So far has He removed our transgressions from us"
(Psalm 103:12). Thank God for providing a gracious refuge from
sin's punishment.

Joshua 21

*All the cities of the Levites in the midst of the possession of the sons of
Israel were forty-eight cities with their pasture lands. —Joshua 21:41*

After the Israelites inhabited the land of Canaan, Joshua divided
the land among all the tribes—except the Levites, who lived scattered throughout the land. They ministered before the Lord and
took care of His tabernacle and its furnishings (Numbers 1:50).
But they also had other responsibilities that made their dwelling throughout the land very important. The Levites counseled
the Israelites in civil and religious affairs, and they assisted the
priests in the worship of God (8:19). Not only did the Levites
serve the Lord and His people, they belonged to God (3:12). Like
the Levites, Christians belong to God and will receive an eternal
inheritance from the Lord (1 Peter 1:3–5). As God's royal priest-
hood and holy people, believers in Christ should scatter among
friends, relatives, and coworkers and provide godly service and
counsel that will draw them toward their heavenly Father (2:9).

Joshua 22

*"And now the LORD your God has given rest to your brothers, as He
spoke to them; therefore turn now and go to your tents, to the land
of your possession, which Moses the servant of the LORD gave you
beyond the Jordan."* —Joshua 22:4

The Reubenites, the Gadites, and the half-tribe of Manasseh
received their inheritance on the east side of the Jordan. But

before they settled down, unpacked, and enjoyed their land, they joined their brothers—all the other tribes and the other half of Manasseh—as they took over the land west of the Jordan. The Reubenites, Gadites, and half-tribe of Manasseh risked their lives and battled the Canaanites so that their fellow Israelites could occupy their trans-Jordan home. And after God gave His people rest, the two-and-a-half tribes journeyed back across the Jordan to enjoy their land. They selflessly helped their brothers just as Moses had commanded them. God has set the standard of selfless service. God the Father sent His Son to bear the sin of the world. And God the Son humbled Himself, took on humanity, and reconciled us to the Father. God expects Christians to serve others with the same generous, sacrificial love. (Philippians 2:3–8)

Joshua 23

"But you are to cling to the LORD your God, as you have done to this day."   *—Joshua 23:8*

What does it mean to "cling to the Lord"? Joshua knew that his days were drawing to a close. In his farewell address, he encouraged the Israelites to remember God's faithfulness, to obey His Law, and to cling to Him. Just as small children hold tightly to their dads' hands when they are scared, God's people were to hold tightly to their Lord. If they firmly grasped the Lord's love, faithfulness, and Law, they wouldn't have room in their hands for anything else. But if they loosened their grip on God, they would become susceptible to pride, selfishness, and idolatry. The same is true today. When Christians forget that the Lord's way is the best way and that there is no replacement for focused obedience and simple faith, spiritual devastation is just around the corner.

Let's cling to the Lord by loving Him, worshiping Him, and trusting His perfect plan.

Joshua 24

Joshua said to all the people, "Thus says the LORD, the God of Israel, 'From ancient times your fathers lived beyond the River, namely, Terah, the father of Abraham and the father of Nahor, and they served other gods.'" —Joshua 24:2

Before Joshua's death, he encouraged the Israelites to remember where they came from. When the Lord first visited Abraham, he and his whole family served false gods. But the Lord told Abraham to leave his people and travel to the land God would give him. And Abraham obeyed; he left behind the idols and followed God. Fast forward to Joshua's final words. When the Israelites entered the land God promised to Abraham, a land with abundant natural resources, Joshua told them to remember God's grace to Abraham and to shun the idolatry from which He had delivered Abraham. Just like the Israelites, Christians need to remember where we came from and how far God has brought us. The Lord has delivered us from such struggles as despair, addiction, loneliness, and idolatry, as well as from the eternal punishment our sin deserves. And He has given us hope, power through the Holy Spirit, friendship, and forgiveness. Thank the Lord for His grace today!

1.   Adapted from Wayne Stiles, *Going Places with God: A Devotional Journey Through the Lands of the Bible* (Ventura, Ca.: Regal Books), 97.

Judges

Judges 1

The spies saw a man coming out of the city and they said to him,
"Please show us the entrance to the city and we will treat you kindly."
                                                              —*Judges 1:24*

As God's people transitioned to living in the Promised Land, they faced the prospect of continued battles with the Canaanites they had failed to remove from the land. As the descendants of Joseph looked to take the prominent city of Bethel, they met a non-Israelite outside the city walls. Though God's people were technically in opposition to this man and his people, they offered the man kindness—for inside information about the city, the Israelites would let the man and his family go free. Israel had a mandate from God to act as His arm of judgment on the Canaanites and to take over the land. But that mandate did not prevent the Israelites from showing kindness to helpful individuals. If God's people could show kindness in the midst of a life-and-death battle for territory, we too should show kindness in a much more open and free environment.

Judges 2

"Therefore I also said, 'I will not drive them out before you; but they
will become as thorns in your sides and their gods will be a snare
to you.'"   —*Judges 2:3*

The book of Judges records the lasting legacy of Israel's failure to remove the Canaanites from the Promised Land. God's people faced seemingly endless confrontations with their enemies living among and around them. God had sent Israel into the Promised Land, not just for Israel's own benefit but also as an instrument of

God's judgment against the Canaanite people and their destructive idolatry. As a means of judgment, however, Israel was largely a failure. While God's people did indeed conquer some territory, they left much unconquered. They got comfortable in the new cities they possessed, failing to pursue their enemies even within the boundaries of God's promised inheritance. This disobedience resulted in consequences, as generations of God's people were forced continually to push back against enemy incursions into their territory. Likewise, our own disobedience has the potential to leave lasting consequences to ourselves and our descendants. Israel's failure reminds us just how destructive our sins can be.

Judges 3

Ehud came to him while he was sitting alone in his cool roof chamber. And Ehud said, "I have a message from God for you." And he arose from his seat. Ehud stretched out his left hand, took the sword from his right thigh and thrust it into his belly.   —*Judges 3:20–21*

In Old Testament times and in the era of the apostles, God regularly used prophets to communicate to people—sometimes to Israel, sometimes to other individuals or nations. Occasionally, these prophets brought messages of hope, but often they carried messages of doom. Announcements of judgment were more common because the people needed them. When the nation of Moab oppressed Israel not long after God's people settled the land, God sent Moab's king a message, but one without words. Ehud's assassination of Moab's king delivered a message of judgment. Messages from God are not always pleasant, and treating His Word as though it always should be pleasant ignores the fullness of God's character and the depths of our own sin. We often

21

need a hard word or startling event to push us back on track, and Ehud's act of judgment upon Moab's king serves as just that.

Judges 4

Now Deborah, a prophetess, the wife of Lappidoth, was judging
Israel at that time. —*Judges 4:4*

During the era of the judges, Israel found itself in desperate need of competent leadership. The people were constantly abandoning the ways of God and were instead practicing idolatry. In the midst of this decaying culture, God chose another judge to lead the people out of foreign bondage. But this time, the judge was different than those He had chosen in the past. This time, He chose a woman. Think about how stunning that would have been in the patriarchal ancient world. In the eyes of people so accustomed to male leadership, Deborah would have seemed a flawed choice. And yet, God used her courage and leadership to deliver His people from Jabin the king of Canaan. God used another woman, Jael, to kill Sisera, the commander of Jabin's army (Judges 4:21). Though society may place constraints on individuals for one reason or another, God can use anyone He chooses, no matter how society views that person.

Judges 5

Then Deborah and Barak the son of Abinoam sang on that day,
saying . . . —*Judges 5:1*

The bulk of Judges 5 records a song that God's people sang upon the defeat of Jabin the king of Canaan. The song recounts the major events and players in the battle. It includes references to the difficult days before Deborah's leadership (Judges 5:6–8). It chronicles the death of Sisera at the hands of a woman, Jael, who used a tent peg to kill the commander of Jabin's army (5:24–26). And it paints the tragic picture of Sisera's mother, waiting for her son to arrive home, though he never would (5:28). Ancient people told their stories in songs, which made the stories easier to remember. But it also placed those stories into the hearts of the people. As a result, the stories helped shape the identities of God's people. Which songs shape our identities today? Make them songs that tell us the truth about ourselves, our world, and our God.

Judges 6

So Israel was brought very low because of Midian, and the sons of Israel cried to the LORD. —Judges 6:6

During one of Israel's forays into idolatry, the Lord used the Midianites to judge His people. This foreign nation joined with the Amalekites and invaded Israel, pillaging and looting crops and livestock. The result for Israel? Utter devastation. Having cast off their spiritual sustenance when they turned to idols, the people of Israel found themselves without physical sustenance also. The writer of Judges stated that these invasions by the Midianites brought the people "very low." It refers not just to their physical poverty but to their spiritual poverty as well. And in that lowly state, God's people humbled themselves and called upon the Lord for help. Often, we have to be brought low in suffering and trials before we recognize our dependence upon God. At our lowest, we feel the pain of lack in our lives. God desires that we seek to replenish with the only One who can provide for our deepest needs—physically and spiritually.

Judges 7

The LORD said to Gideon, "The people who are with you are too many for Me to give Midian into their hands, for Israel would become boastful, saying, 'My own power has delivered me.'" —Judges 7:2

When the Lord answered Israel's call to come to their aid against the raids by the Midianites, He made Gideon His judge to lead an army of the people into battle against their foes. God had a clear motive both in His choice of Gideon as well as in His choice of the particular fighters in Gideon's army. The Lord wanted the people to understand that their deliverance came as a result of His power, not their own. To make this abundantly clear, God chose as His leader a weak man given to idolatry, as well as a miniscule army to fight the powerful Midianite forces. The story of Gideon and his army reveals to us one of God's favorite ways of working: illustrating His power through human weakness. When we are weak, He is strong. When we fail, His grace is sufficient for us (2 Corinthians 12:9).

Judges 8

But Gideon said to them, "I will not rule over you, nor shall my son rule over you; the LORD shall rule over you." Yet Gideon said to them, "I would request of you, that each of you give me an earring from his spoil." (For they had gold earrings, because they were Ishmaelites.) —Judges 8:23–24

After Gideon and his army defeated the Midianites, the people revered the flawed leader. They asked Gideon to go beyond his specific God-given task of delivering the people and become their full-time ruler—a request Gideon denied (Judges 8:22–23). Gideon understood that God ruled over the people of Israel and that no man should aspire to be their king. However, he used his position to surpass the limited role God had given him by asking the people to contribute gold jewelry. The people enthusiastically donated to this project, and Gideon took the gold, melted it down, and fashioned an ephod. With the aid of this golden garment worn by priests in worship, the people—Gideon included—fell into idolatry. Gideon used his influence to insert elements of idol worship into the life of Israel. We must all take care that our own desires or innovations regarding worship are consistent with godliness, lest we lead others astray.

Judges 9

"Speak, now, in the hearing of all the leaders of Shechem, 'Which is better for you, that seventy men, all the sons of Jerubbaal, rule over you, or that one man rule over you?' Also, remember that I am your bone and your flesh."   —*Judges 9:2*

After Gideon's death, his son Abimelech sought to capitalize on his heritage. Abimelech schemed to become the ruler over God's people. He appealed to his closest relatives for support, then used that support to kill nearly all of his seventy brothers and half-brothers (Judges 9:5). That God allowed Abimelech to rule three years and used him to defeat some of Israel's enemies shows the magnificence of God's grace. Ultimately, however, we should see Abimelech's life as a cautionary tale. Abimelech did exactly what his father had refused to do—he assumed a position of power over God's people, displacing God as Israel's ruler. In our pride, we often do something similar. Are we denying the authority of our Creator as our ruler, thus following Abimelech and Israel into the grave sin of idolatry? We must humbly follow God's direction for our lives, rather than set up ourselves as rulers of our own lives.

Judges 10

Then the sons of Israel cried out to the LORD, saying, "We have sinned against You, for indeed, we have forsaken our God and served the Baals." . . . So they put away the foreign gods from among them and served the LORD; and He could bear the misery of Israel no longer.
—Judges 10:10, 16

God often waits on our repentance before He acts on our behalf. In the years after Tola's time as judge over Israel, the people once again fell into idolatry and faced oppression. But when they first cried out to God, He refused to deliver them. They had neither turned away from their idolatry nor grappled with God's repeated deliverance in the past (Judges 10:12–13). That God waits on His people to repent before He delivers them goes to show the foundational importance of repentance in the lives of God's people. We cannot experience true deliverance without turning from our lives of sin. In this way, repentance becomes much more than a change of mind; it is a complete change of orientation. God eventually delivered the people of Israel but only after they had made staggering changes in their lives—putting away idols and actively serving God with their lives (Judges 10:16).

Judges 11

Now Jephthah the Gileadite was a valiant warrior, but he was the son of a harlot. And Gilead was the father of Jephthah. Gilead's wife bore him sons; and when his wife's sons grew up, they drove Jephthah out and said to him, "You shall not have an inheritance in our father's house, for you are the son of another woman." —Judges 11:1–2

The judge Jephthah owed his existence to the sinful union between his father and a harlot. And his origin cast a shadow over his life, both in the wider community and in his own home. After Jephthah's father sired children with his wife, those children eventually hated their older half-brother and forced him from the family abode. One sexual sin by Jephthah's father, Gilead, led to poisonous family connections. Though blood-related, no longer would these people live together. The Lord's boundaries for sexual purity within marriage are meant to protect us from the pain and hardship that often come out of situations like Jephthah's. When fathers or mothers choose sin over righteousness, the consequences ripple outward, impacting not just the parents but the children as well. Jephthah's divided family continues to serve as a pertinent warning, especially given the prevalence of sexual sin and divorce that plague God's people today.

Judges 12

Then Jephthah gathered all the men of Gilead and fought Ephraim; and the men of Gilead defeated Ephraim, because they said, "You are fugitives of Ephraim, O Gileadites, in the midst of Ephraim and in the midst of Manasseh." —Judges 12:4

Israel's entry into the Promised Land carried with it a sense of triumph. God opened the way for the people to take their inheritance, to overcome their enemies. However, in the centuries that followed, the people's faithfulness to God plummeted, eventually leading them to fights, not just with their enemies but among themselves as well. After Jephthah defeated the Ammonites, the people of Ephraim complained that the judge had not brought them along (Judges 12:1). This led to a conflict within Israel. Ultimately, the military strength of the Gileadites under Jepthath overcame that of Ephraim, leaving forty-two thousand Ephraimites dead. Civil war in the midst of Jephthah's judgeship revealed the depths of Israel's wickedness—not even God's judge brought peace to their land any longer. When a nation, a community, or a family can no longer live at peace with itself, no one wins. One side might be right, but both suffer the tragedy of fighting their own.

Judges 13

For it came about when the flame went up from the altar toward heaven, that the angel of the LORD ascended in the flame of the altar. When Manoah and his wife saw this, they fell on their faces to the ground.
—Judges 13:20

As Israel sunk once again into sin and bondage—this time to the Philistines—God made Himself known in an out-of-the-way village to an unknown couple. Manoah and his (unnamed) wife had been barren, a state viewed by people in those days as a sure sign of God's disfavor. Into this dark corner, God shined the light of revelation, assuring this longsuffering couple through the angel of the Lord that they would bear a son who would grow to become Israel's deliverer (Judges 13:5). Manoah and his wife found hope of renewal in the news of their coming child. At times of great darkness, we do well to look for signs of God's care for the world. Though we may not receive angelic revelation, the whole of creation testifies to God's presence (Romans 1:20). Even with the world at its darkest, God dwells with His people, working out His plans for our good.

Judges 14

However, his father and mother did not know that it was of the LORD, for He was seeking an occasion against the Philistines. Now at that time the Philistines were ruling over Israel. —Judges 14:4

Samson grew up as a Nazirite (Judges 13:5). This special way of life, which included avoiding wine and dead bodies (Numbers 6:3–8), symbolized God's separateness from the people. So when Samson told his parents that he wanted to marry a Philistine woman, likely they were stunned. Not only was Samson living as a Nazirite, but the people of God as a whole were to be separate, or holy, unto God. Marriage with a nonbeliever was out of the question. And yet, based on God's previous revelation that Samson would deliver Israel from the Philistines, God intended to use Samson's weakness for foreign women as a means of Israel's deliverance. God often works through our weaknesses. Certainly, we need not indulge those weaknesses. But neither should a failure convince us that God is finished with us, for He receives His greatest glory when working through our frailty.

Judges 15

*He found a fresh jawbone of a donkey, so he reached out and took it
and killed a thousand men with it.* —Judges 15:15

The conflict between Samson and the Philistines began in rela-
tion to Samson's Philistine wife. The Philistines lined up for war
against Judah after Samson killed a large group of Philistines
in revenge (Judges 15:8–10). When the people of Judah, out
of fear, delivered Samson over to the Philistines, he broke his
bonds, picked up the jawbone of a donkey, and killed one thousand Philistines with it (15:13–15). God often works through
the most unsuspecting of instruments. Most people in Judah or
Philistia would not have felt emboldened or endangered by the
presence of a dead donkey's jawbone, yet God used that small
piece of bone to bring His people relief. The donkey's jawbone
reminds us that God works through all kinds of people and
objects. We might be small or unknown, but that does not prevent God from using us to reveal His power and His ability to
save others from darkness.

Judges 16

*Then she said to him, "How can you say, 'I love you,' when your
heart is not with me? You have deceived me these three times and
have not told me where your great strength is."* —Judges 16:15

The story of Samson and Delilah reveals the tragic consequences
of manipulation. Delilah didn't deal honestly with Samson,
continuing their relationship out of a desire for information
rather than for something lasting and true. Delilah eventually
received her information, which resulted in the torture and death
of Samson, as well as the deaths of three thousand Philistines.

While not all manipulation leads to physical death, it does open the path toward the death of real love and lasting relationships. The manipulator lives a lie, showing a false interest in real relationship while seeking to exert control over another person. True love, however, doesn't involve manipulation. Delilah manipulated because she was more faithful to her own people than to her lover. Further, by manipulating Samson, Delilah set herself against God, as she used falsehood to undermine God's people. In the same way, when we manipulate, we use a tool of the Father of Lies to achieve our own ends.

Judges 17

So Micah consecrated the Levite, and the young man became his priest and lived in the house of Micah.   —Judges 17:12

Already established as a thief and an idolater, Micah took advantage of an out-of-work priest, offering him the security of a paying job (Judges 17:10). The wandering Levite accepted the position to "lead worship" at Micah's personal shrine, even though it meant compromising the worship of the true God. That the priest was wandering unsupported by the people and that he was willing to forego the true worship of God offers contemporary readers a sense of how far the nation had fallen. Without proper support from the people to lead worship at the temple consistent with God's desires, priests became desperately hungry and were willing to do whatever it took to get a meal. We must take care to offer proper support to the good and faithful spiritual leaders God has placed in our midst. When we do not, we risk devolving into disconnected and strictly personalized worship of gods of our own making.

Judges 18

Now the five men who went to spy out the land went up and entered there, and took the graven image and the ephod and household idols and the molten image, while the priest stood by the entrance of the gate with the six hundred men armed with weapons of war.

—Judges 18:17

After Joshua died, the tribe of Dan never properly settled into their God-given inheritance. This led the Danites to spy out another area. On the way to invade the peaceful city of Laish, the Danites stole Micah's idol and kidnapped his priest, taking by force for themselves that which was evil (Judges 18:17–20). Not only had the people begun to fight among themselves and to drift from the true worship of God, they now stole to enhance their idolatry. What started with a simple story of idolatry involving one man, Micah, had expanded to include a priest and an entire tribe of Israel. The national implications of idolatry are unmistakable in this passage—what the people do, the community will become. Our actions are never just our own. They have profound effects on those around us. The account of the Danites should remind us to keep our worship and our deeds focused upon and in service to the true God.

Judges 19

But the men would not listen to him. So the man seized his concubine and brought her out to them; and they raped her and abused her all night until morning, then let her go at the approach of dawn.

—Judges 19:25

At this point in history, Israel's priests were not only involved in idolatry (Judges 17), they were also taking concubines for themselves (19:1). Judges 19 records one such priest on a journey with his concubine. Stopping to stay the night at Gibeah, the priest encountered a group of men who wanted to rape him (19:22). Instead, the priest offered up his concubine, whom the men abused and left for dead. She died alone and outdoors, without anyone to care for her wounds. The Levite priest cared for this woman only as an object of sexual satisfaction, not as a creation of God imbued with inherent dignity. Our treatment of women stands as a marker for our spiritual condition. We must guard against the temptation to objectify women. When we worship the Creator and turn our attention away from ourselves, we will have a wonderful foundation upon which to treat women—and all people—with dignity and respect.

Judges 20

"Now then, deliver up the men, the worthless fellows in Gibeah, that we may put them to death and remove this wickedness from Israel." But the sons of Benjamin would not listen to the voice of their brothers, the sons of Israel. —*Judges 20:13*

Pride often prevents us from doing what's best for others. It leads us to think first of our own interests while shutting our ears to the interests of others. After the incident in Gibeah with the rape and murder of the Levite's concubine, the nation came upon the city looking for justice (Judges 20:9). Though there was no doubt that the woman died violently in Gibeah, the people of the city refused to give up the culprits. This led to a battle between Israel and the tribe of Benjamin (where Gibeah was located). Forty thousand Israelites died in the three day conflict, while the army of Benjamin was decimated. The prideful harboring of wrongdoers in Gibeah led to death on a grand scale. The tribe of

Benjamin fought their Israelite brothers to defend an injustice. Such misplaced priorities might leave our pride intact, but they also deliver to our doorsteps injury and death.

Judges 21

In those days there was no king in Israel; everyone did what was right in his own eyes. —Judges 21:25

The final verse of Judges articulates the tragic early history of Israel in the Promised Land. Israelite culture had become completely saturated with the pursuit of selfish desires. God's people had gone from having admirable leaders willing to defend their people to having compromised leaders and priests willing to sacrifice the lives of their own to protect self-serving ideals. They took what they wanted in life. Such a people could only be led by brute force, because such a people would not have it any other way. Therefore, if they were to have a king, he would have to compel their allegiance by forceful measures (taxing the people, conscripting young men for the army, and so on). Today, the Spirit gives God's people freedom to choose goodness over selfishness. But living that choice requires a countercultural approach to life that eschews common comforts and the status quo in favor of sacrificial acts for the good of others.

Ruth

Ruth 1

Then she arose with her daughters-in-law that she might return from the land of Moab, for she had heard in the land of Moab that the LORD had visited His people in giving them food.   —Ruth 1:6

Escaping the famine in Bethlehem, Naomi's family fled to Moab against the will of God. And they stayed for ten years. In Moab, Naomi's husband died, then her two sons died and her life became barren. So she departed from that place and returned to the land of Judah. Naomi changed the direction of her life, leaving the path her husband had taken. Was she fearful of her reception in Bethlehem? Would they accept her back with open arms? It didn't matter. Nervous or not, she set her foot toward home. She returned to the Lord's land. Guilt, fear, and shame often immobilize us. One step into sin brings shameful thoughts that we have gone too far to change. But even when we're outside God's will, we can always return to the Lord. Naomi had been in a land she was not called to, and she lost everything. But we, like Naomi, can always turn around.

Ruth 2

And Ruth the Moabitess said to Naomi, "Please let me go to the field and glean among the ears of grain after one in whose sight I may find favor. And she said to her, "Go, my daughter."   —Ruth 2:2

Ruth asked permission to collect grain left by the reapers after the harvest, an act performed by foreigners and the poor. God had commanded that farmers leave the corners of the fields untouched for the needy widows, orphans, and slaves to glean (Leviticus 23:22). And Ruth diligently went to the fields to gather for herself and her mother-in-law . . . without complaining. She was hopeful, even after losing a husband and moving to a foreign land. In contrast to Naomi, who declared her bitterness to the Lord, Ruth did not dwell on the loss and suffering she had endured in her young life (Ruth 1:20–21). Instead, she humbly sought to provide for Naomi. We all can think of reasons to be bitter. Ruth's example reminds us to change our perspective from one of resentment to one of humility and trust in God's plan. In the end, God's plan for Ruth was more blessed than any she could have imagined.

Ruth 3

Then he said, "May you be blessed of the Lord, my daughter. You have shown your last kindness to be better than the first by not going after young men, whether poor or rich." —Ruth 3:10

Ruth could have married a younger man. But she was faithful to the Law of God and the right of the kinsman-redeemer—which allowed a brother (or other near relative) to marry a widowed sister-in-law and provide for her (Deuteronomy 25:5–10). Ruth first showed kindness to Naomi, but Boaz saw Ruth's willingness to marry him as an even greater kindness—his lineage would continue. This sincere kindness made a lasting impact on Boaz. First impressions are essential. Entire relationships are often built upon first impressions, and we have all felt the pressure to make them positive and authentic. But do we strive to make our next impression—or our last impression—as sincere as the first? Do our efforts continue so that the Lord may be glorified in every action? Following the example of Ruth, we must pursue relationships with as much integrity as we strived for in the beginning.

Ruth 4

All the people who were in the court, and the elders, said, "We are witnesses. May the LORD make the woman who is coming into your home like Rachel and Leah, both of whom built the house of Israel; and may you achieve wealth in Ephrathah and become famous in Bethlehem."
                                                                    —Ruth 4:11

Boaz was a law-abiding Israelite. Ruth was a Moabite. The Law forbade Moabites from entering the assembly of the Lord (Deuteronomy 23:3, 6). Yet Boaz married Ruth. He looked at the intent of the Law, recognized God's redemption of Ruth, accepted her as his own, and displayed the loyal love of God. Through Boaz, God provided Ruth a home and a family. God's desire is for all people to be brought into relationship with Him. Boaz understood this, and because Ruth believed in Yahweh, she was welcomed into the community. She became part of the house of Israel, like Rachel and Leah, and a part of Christ's lineage. In our own lives, we must remember to look for God's plan and accept into Christian fellowship those who have been redeemed, whether or not they meet our approval.

First Samuel

1 Samuel 1

But to Hannah he would give a double portion, for he loved Hannah, but the LORD had closed her womb. —1 Samuel 1:5

Babies are born every day. They are, in fact, born by the thousands. Though some are not, many of them are wanted and viewed as significant in the eyes of their parents. Many of them are even unplanned, but they are accepted as special, unique vessels given by the hand of God—like Hannah's son, Samuel. Hannah was the wife of a man named Elkanah. She shared Elkanah with a woman named Peninnah. Peninnah had children. Hannah had none. The Lord had closed her womb. Why? Because God is sovereign. Hannah trusted in God and "prayed to the Lord and wept bitterly" (1 Samuel 1:10). And in God's timing, Hannah conceived. So how can Christians follow Hannah's faithful example? By acknowledging God's sovereign plan, by persisting in prayer, and by accepting God's delays and God's surprises. As believers, we should remember that all children—even the most unexpected—are significant in God's plan for the future.

1 Samuel 2

Now the sons of Eli were worthless men; they did not know the LORD. —1 Samuel 2:12

Being the high priest, Eli went in once a year to the holiest place in the tabernacle. No one else in the land had that privilege. He was working with the people in spiritual things, addressing their needs, giving counsel, and spending his time in the place of worship. But how about his boys? This may surprise you. They were immoral reprobates and spiritual losers! Though priests, they despised the sacrifices of God and took sexual advantage of the women who came in for worship. And here's another surprise: Eli knew it. God would not simply cover His eyes concerning their sin; He would bring about swift consequences. As Christian parents, we shouldn't fold our arms and think, *I just can't do a thing with these kids!* And we certainly can't say, "I'm too busy to discipline my kids; surely God will understand." No, God won't understand! Parents, we are accountable to fulfill our responsibilities with honor and integrity.

1 Samuel 3

Then the LORD came and stood and called as at other times, "Samuel! Samuel!" And Samuel said, "Speak, for Your servant is listening."
—1 Samuel 3:10

The Lord spoke audibly to Samuel, the very young assistant to Eli, the high priest. The message Samuel was to give Eli was one of the most severe warnings God had ever issued. God said, "I have sworn to the house of Eli that the iniquity of Eli's house shall not be atoned for by sacrifice or offering forever" (1 Samuel 3:14). The message was a huge burden for little Samuel, but it was not something Eli hadn't already heard. God had pulled Eli aside on previous occasions and told him about his wayward sons. (Please stop and read 1 Samuel 2:27–32.) But Eli failed to heed God's warning. As Christians, we should learn from Eli and remember that merely hearing the truth isn't enough. Action is essential. Faith is an action. That means God's blessings almost always lie on the other side of obedience. According to Scripture, knowledge alone merely puffs up, but with action comes humility.

1 Samuel 4

And the ark of God was taken; and the two sons of Eli, Hophni and Phinehas, died.   —1 Samuel 4:11

Ignoring sin inevitably leads to severe consequences. Though Eli knew that his sons were disobedient, he did not directly confront them. His sons were carnal and lustful men, and yet they went right on practicing the things of God. As a result, God promised to punish them with death (1 Samuel 2:25). Eli said to his sons, "Why do you do such things, the evil things that I hear from all these people?" (1 Samuel 2:23). But Eli's approach was wrong because what his sons were doing was, to him, hearsay. Eli did not know his sons well enough to discipline them properly. As parents, we must study our children so that we know them inside and out. If we are not consistent in loving and faithfully disciplining our children, they will rise up and curse us by—or before—the end of our days. Furthermore, without proper correction, their sin may very well end up destroying their lives.

1 Samuel 5

Therefore neither the priests of Dagon nor all who enter Dagon's house tread on the threshold of Dagon in Ashdod to this day.
                                        —1 Samuel 5:5

God will not share His glory with anyone or anything else. When the Philistines captured the ark of the covenant from Israel and placed it in the temple of Dagon, their false god, the Lord was not pleased. So God rebuked the Philistines in a very memorable way. The morning after they put the ark in Dagon's temple, the Philistines found their idol face down before the ark. Blinded to the Lord's supernatural intervention, the Philistines put Dagon back where he had been. But the next morning they found a decapitated Dagon, with no hands, lying prostrate before God's ark. Believers in Christ must be careful not to place any idols—money, employment, relationships, material items—in our hearts. Like a headless, handless statue, these things we worship are impotent and ignorant. Only God can love us, guide us, and fulfill His plans in our lives. The Lord alone deserves our exclusive adoration.

1 Samuel 6

And the cows took the straight way in the direction of Beth-shemesh; they went along the highway, lowing as they went, and did not turn aside to the right or to the left. And the lords of the Philistines followed them to the border of Beth-shemesh.   —1 Samuel 6:12

After the Philistines captured God's ark, they put it in the temple of their idol, Dagon. But after God made a mockery of their false god and plagued the Philistines with tumors and mice, they decided to get rid of the ark before any more judgments fell on them. They put the ark and a guilt offering of gold on a cart and hitched it to a couple of cows. Then the Philistines let them go and watched as the cows marched straight back to Israel on their own. So what lessons can Christians learn from a couple of cows? Those cows obeyed God, they knew their destination, and they didn't deviate from the path. As believers, we show the Lord that we love Him by obeying Him. And as walk the path of obedience, we will reach our ultimate goal—to glorify Him.

1 Samuel 7

Then Samuel took a stone and set it between Mizpah and Shen, and named it Ebenezer, saying, "Thus far the Lord has helped us."
—*1 Samuel 7:12*

"Here I raise mine Ebenezer; hither by thy help I'm come." Ever wonder what this line means as you sing the eighteenth-century hymn "Come, Thou Fount"? What in the world is an Ebenezer? As the Israelites faced the threat of the Philistines, they trembled with fear. So Samuel prayed to the Lord and asked Him to defeat the Philistines. God answered Samuel with a thunderstorm that disoriented and defeated the Philistine army. In order to commemorate God's answer to prayer, Samuel set up a stone memorial between Mizpah and Shen and called it *Ebenezer*, which means "stone of help." Samuel wanted the Israelites to celebrate the Lord's help and always to remember to depend on Him for deliverance from their enemies. God still helps His people today. As Christians who pray to the Lord and watch Him respond with provision, protection, and guidance, we can set up "memorial stones" in our minds so we might never forget how God has helped us.

1 Samuel 8

The Lord said to Samuel, "Listen to the voice of the people in regard to all that they say to you, for they have not rejected you, but they have rejected Me from being king over them."   —*1 Samuel 8:7*

People have always wanted to be like everybody else, to do the popular thing. The ancient Israelites were no exception. In essence, they were saying, "We're tired of worshiping an invisible

God. Nobody else does! Everybody says, 'Where's your king?' We want a human leader here on earth, like all the other nations." So God let them have exactly what they wanted. The man they chose, Saul, was tall, dark, and handsome. That's how people choose kings. Saul had a measure of humility to begin with and seemed able to rally people around a cause. But before long, he became thin-skinned, hot-tempered, and given to deep valleys of depression, including thoughts of murder. So much for the man who was the people's choice! When we don't wait on God to provide what we need, we usually take matters into our own hands. As a result, we become disillusioned with the choices we have made. But graciously, God doesn't abandon us when we make bad choices. He intervenes.

1 Samuel 9

Saul replied, "Am I not a Benjamite, of the smallest of the tribes of Israel, and my family the least of all the families of the tribe of Benjamin? Why then do you speak to me in this way?"

— *1 Samuel 9.21*

When we acknowledge who we are and don't pretend to be someone we're not, that's humility. That's how Saul started. When his father's donkeys got lost, Saul went on a mission to find them. On his way, Saul met Samuel, who had received directions from the Lord to anoint Saul as king. When Samuel asked Saul to dine with him, Saul wondered why. Saul knew he didn't come from the most prominent family in the biggest tribe. He knew he didn't deserve the honor he was receiving. As Christians acknowledge who we are before God, we can serve Him freely so that He gets all the glory. As God's servants, we should have one great goal — to help others see God's power, His grace, His love, and His justice. Instead of pointing to our own gifts, talents, and accomplishments, we can acknowledge God as the giver of those gifts and point others to Him.

1 Samuel 10

So they ran and took him from there, and when he stood among the people, he was taller than any of the people from his shoulders upward. —1 Samuel 10:23

Nothing can replace character. Samuel was a godly man, so the nation of Israel had hope and motivation, and they pursued purity. They had a leader they could trust. Integrity characterized Samuel's leadership. But when the Israelites asked for a king, they forgot about honesty, morality, and courage. They accepted Saul as king because he was good-looking and towered over everyone else (1 Samuel 10:23). His size fooled the Israelites into thinking he could be a good king. But because he lacked integrity, it wasn't long before the people witnessed his lack of character. Even though he had all the external qualifications, people started to distrust him, and national morale tanked. When choosing leaders, Christians must always value honesty above showmanship, and character over charisma. And when fulfilling leadership roles, believers in Christ must put more time into developing godly character than polishing our image and delivering slick speeches. In God's eyes, faithfulness and integrity define success.

1 Samuel 11

Then the Spirit of God came upon Saul mightily when he heard these
words, and he became very angry. — *1 Samuel 11:6*

When the Ammonites attacked the inhabitants of Jabesh-gilead
and threatened to gouge out their eyes in exchange for a truce,
King Saul became furious. But his anger didn't result from selfishness or fear; the Spirit of God came on Saul and made him
feel God's anger. So King Saul rallied the Israelite army to fight
against the Ammonites. Saul chopped up a couple of oxen and
sent pieces throughout Israel, threatening to slaughter the oxen
of Israelites who refused to fight for their brothers in Jabesh-
gilead. When the Holy Spirit works in a believer's life, sometimes
He inspires righteous anger. Human beings have the capacity to
experience emotions, including anger, because God created us in
His image. When Jesus, the God-Man, entered the temple and
witnessed the rich exploiting the poor for profit, He got mad
(John 2:13–17)! We, too, need to become angry at the things
that make God angry.

1 Samuel 12

"Now, here is the king walking before you, but I am old and gray, and
behold my sons are with you. And I have walked before you from my
youth even to this day." — *1 Samuel 12:2*

Samuel put a crown on Saul's head, backed away, and delivered his swan song. National trust was at its highest level, not
because of the new king but because of the old judge, Samuel,
who plugged away and did his job unto God. Saul was not qualified, and it broke the heart of Samuel, but he said, "Go ahead."

Even after Samuel had condemned the people's sin and severely warned them, he stayed committed to them and to doing what was right. "Far be it from me that I should sin against the LORD by ceasing to pray for you; but I will instruct you in the good and right way" (1 Samuel 12:23). Samuel had faithfully served God, day in and day out, and that's what made him a great leader. Christians must remember that when God looks for leaders, He is not looking for magnificent specimens of humanity. He's looking for deeply committed, genuinely humble, honest-to-the-core servants.

1 Samuel 13

"But now your kingdom shall not endure. The LORD has sought out for Himself a man after His own heart, and the LORD has appointed him as ruler over His people, because you have not kept what the LORD commanded you." — 1 Samuel 13:14

When God scans the earth for potential leaders, He is not on a search for angels in the flesh. He is certainly not looking for perfect people, since there are none. He is searching for men and women with certain qualities, like those He found in David. The Lord had gone to the home of Jesse on a secret surveillance mission. And He noticed in David an important quality: *spirituality*. David was a person whose life was in harmony with the Lord. What is important to Him was important to David. What burdens the Lord's heart burdened David's heart. So what does *spirituality* look like for Christians today? That means there are no locked closets. Nothing's been swept under the rugs. That means that when Christians do wrong, we admit it and immediately come to terms with it. God is looking for men and women whose hearts are completely His.

1 Samuel 14

Then Jonathan said to the young man who was carrying his armor,
"Come and let us cross over to the garrison of these uncircumcised;
perhaps the LORD will work for us, for the LORD is not restrained to
save by many or by few." —1 Samuel 14:6

Jonathan knew that with the Lord on his side, he could overcome insurmountable odds. But the biggest obstacle Jonathan had to overcome was not the Philistine garrison that he and his armor bearer planned to attack, but his father's fear. King Saul saw the huge Philistine military, armed with thirty thousand chariots and six thousand horsemen (1 Samuel 13:5), and Saul led the Israelite army to retreat into hiding. Finally, after Jonathan had had enough of his father's inactivity, he and his armor bearer attacked the Philistines. Jonathan trusted that with the Lord on his side, even a huge army didn't have a chance! Followers of Jesus Christ should remember that fear often prevents us from experiencing God's powerful work on our behalf. Whether we fear poverty, sickness, or a risky opportunity to serve God, the Lord will give us strength to trust Him. Don't let fear, which is the enemy of faith, result in inactivity.

1 Samuel 15

Then Saul said to Samuel, "I have sinned; I have indeed transgressed
the command of the LORD and your words, because I feared the
people and listened to their voice." —1 Samuel 15:24

King Saul was a real piece of work. After he became king of Israel, his actions and decisions soon revealed to the people that he wasn't the man they thought he was. He was, instead, a selfish, angry, hateful, mean-spirited man. During the later years of his rule he lost touch with reality, thus disqualifying himself for the job. Early in Saul's regime, when God commanded him to kill all the Amalekites, Saul openly disobeyed God. When Samuel pointed his finger at the king, Saul at first tried to rationalize what he had done, then finally admitted, "I am guilty." But even then, Saul qualified his confession, "because I feared the people and listened to their voice" (1 Samuel 15:24). The tragic story of Saul is that he never, ever fully repented of his sin. Though believers in Christ have received complete forgiveness, unguarded and vulnerable confession to God and others preserves our relationships with the Lord and the people we love.

1 Samuel 16

Then one of the young men said, "Behold, I have seen a son of Jesse the Bethlehemite who is a skillful musician, a mighty man of valor, a warrior, one prudent in speech, and a handsome man; and the LORD is with him."   *— 1 Samuel 16:18*

Early archaeological records, carvings, and inscriptions show us that the ancients believed music soothed passions, healed mental diseases, and even held in check riots and tumults. It is interesting how God used this belief to provide the missing link needed to connect David to Saul and the throne. Saul was depressed and was looking for someone to provide him with soothing music. One of the young men around Saul knew about David and said, "I know a young man who can do that." This story proves that believers should never discount anything in their past. God can pick it up and use it in the most incredible ways. You never know when something that happened years ago will open a door of opportunity. That's precisely what happened to David. God used David's musical skill, which he learned while in the fields of Judea, to connect him with Saul.

1 Samuel 17

But David said to Saul, "Your servant was tending his father's sheep. When a lion or a bear came and took a lamb from the flock, I went out after him and attacked him, and rescued it from his mouth; and when he rose up against me, I seized him by his beard and struck him and killed him." —1 Samuel 17:34–35

Remember Saul? Great big, tall guy? Now he's scared to death, knees knocking, inside his tent, hiding from Goliath. On the other hand, here's little David, saying, "Hey, let's go whip the giant." Where did David get such courage? He had learned it all alone with God. David was a man of reality. Goliath was no big deal because David had been killing lions and bears while nobody was around. He'd been facing reality long before he squared off against Goliath. Somehow we've gotten the idea that "getting alone with God" is unrealistic . . . that it's not the real world. But that's not true. Getting alone with God doesn't mean we find a quiet spot and think about infinity. No, it means we get alone and pray, cultivating inner strength, so we might be more responsible and diligent in *all* the areas of our lives.

1 Samuel 18

Then Saul became very angry, for this saying displeased him; and he said, "They have ascribed to David ten thousands, but to me they have ascribed thousands. Now what more can he have but the kingdom?" —1 Samuel 18:8

Saul's relationship with David deteriorated. Ultimately, Saul despised him. Keep in mind that David had done nothing to deserve the treatment Saul gave him. Saul's jealousy got in the way. First Samuel 18:8 says that "Saul became very angry." The Hebrew word translated "angry" means "to burn within." Saul was fuming. Then, as his fear and worry intensified, Saul became paranoid. So how can Christians handle angry opposition? Remember: being positive and wise is the best reaction to an enemy. When we see our enemy coming, let's not roll up our mental sleeves, looking for ways to retaliate. It's helpful to remember how David handled Saul. David just kept behaving wisely. And when the heat became intolerable, he fled the scene. He refused to fight back or get even. If we're rubbing shoulders with a jealous individual, whether it be a roommate, a boss, a friend, or even a mate, remember the model of David and emulate it.

1 Samuel 19

Then Jonathan spoke well of David to Saul his father and said to him, "Do not let the king sin against his servant David, since he has not sinned against you, and since his deeds have been very beneficial to you." —1 Samuel 19:4

God knew that David needed an intimate friend to walk with him through the long valley that lay ahead of him. An intimate friend is a loyal defense before others. That's what Jonathan was to David. That "Jonathan spoke well of David to Saul his father" (1 Samuel 19:4) was very significant, because Saul was not only the king and Jonathan's father but also, by that time, David's enemy. Yet Jonathan stood up to his father and said, "Dad, you're wrong about David." In fact, Jonathan not only defended his friend, he also rebuked his father for his attitude toward David. What a friend Jonathan was! As Saul's son, he might have been the heir apparent. Instead, Jonathan trusted in God's choice of king. Christians should follow Jonathan's model of faithful friendship. Instead of treating companions with pettiness, envy, and jealousy, believers should stand up for each other as true friends.

1 Samuel 20

Then Jonathan said to David, "Whatever you say, I will do for you."
—1 Samuel 20:4

For many years, David was hunted and haunted by madman Saul. The king's single objective was to kill David. He was determined to finish him off. Between Saul and David, however, stood a sheltering tree named Jonathan, who gave shade and shelter to David in that precarious place. No matter how hard he tried, Saul could not chop down that tree! Loyal and dependable, Jonathan assured David, "Whatever you say, I will do for you" (1 Samuel 20:4). No limits. No conditions. Jonathan "went to David . . . and encouraged him in God" (23:16). Why? Because Jonathan was committed to the basic principles of friendship. We read that "Jonathan loved him as himself" (18:1). Love knit their hearts together—the kind of love that causes men to lay down their lives for their friends, as Jesus put it (John 15:13). No greater love exists on this planet. Are you loving your friends in this way?

1 Samuel 21

So he disguised his sanity before them, and acted insanely in their hands, and scribbled on the doors of the gate, and let his saliva run down into his beard. —1 Samuel 21:13

How much like the tide we are! When our spirits are high, we are flooded with optimism. But when low, with our jagged barnacles of discouragement exposed, we entertain feelings of raw disillusionment. Often, low tides follow acts of great valor. After killing Goliath, David distinguished himself as a brave fighter. But he later became the target of Saul's spear. He was forced to flee. Due to fear and panic, he resorted to acting insane before the Philistine king of Gath. The once-exalted man of valor now "scribbled on the doors of the gate, and let his saliva run down into his beard" (1 Samuel 21:13). What a sight David must have been! He reached low tide. Believers in Christ experience low tides too. But at low tide, God reminds us that we need encouragement from other believers, that we are utterly dependent on God, and that we must trust in the true Source of strength.

1 Samuel 22

So David departed from there and escaped to the cave of Adullam.
—1 Samuel 22:1

David had bottomed out. In a downward swirl of events, he lost his job, his wife, his home, his counselor, his closest friend, and finally his self-respect. Realizing that his identity was known by the Philistines, he feigned insanity and then slipped out of the city of Gath. Once more he was a fugitive on the run. He had no security, no food, no one to talk to, no promise to cling to, and no hope that anything would ever change. He hid alone in a dark cave, away from everything and everybody he loved . . . everybody except God. Sometimes God brings believers to a difficult place so He can truly begin to shape us and prepare us for His use. When the sovereign God brings us to nothing, it is to renew and rebuild our lives, not to end them. How important it is to trust God when the bottom drops out!

1 Samuel 23

David stayed in the wilderness in the strongholds, and remained in
the hill country in the wilderness of Ziph. And Saul sought him every
day, but God did not deliver him into his hand.   *—1 Samuel 23:14*

God was preparing David for a powerful and lengthy reign on the throne of Israel, but David didn't know that. All he knew during these years was that King Saul was dogging his steps every day, stalking his every move, waiting for him to be vulnerable so Saul could wipe him off the earth. In fact, the entire army of Israel was committed to the death of David. So he went into hiding. En Gedi was a perfect hideout for David. It was an oasis in the desert wilderness with freshwater springs, lush vegetation, and countless caves in the rocky limestone cliffs in which he could hide, high above the Dead Sea. In David's time of need, God provided physical protection, water, and a natural lookout spot where David could see for miles. It was an ideal vantage point, where he was able to guard against any enemy's approach. Remember: when the Lord uses difficult circumstances to prepare His children for a future role, He will provide everything we need during the waiting period.

1 Samuel 24

The men of David said to him, "Behold, this is the day of which the LORD said to you, 'Behold; I am about to give your enemy into your hand, and you shall do to him as it seems good to you.'" Then David arose and cut off the edge of Saul's robe secretly. —1 Samuel 24:4

The Bible is a book that depicts real, historical events, and this unique story is living proof. On one occasion, in the midst of his mad rush for vengeance, Saul had to answer the call of nature. So he crouched in the privacy of a cave—but not just any cave. He unknowingly chose the mouth of the cave where David and his men were hiding. Talk about being vulnerable! So what did David do? He snipped off the edge of Saul's robe. But instead of gloating, David became troubled. He began to experience guilt because he had considered harming the Lord's anointed king (1 Samuel 24:5–6). When Christians really want to walk with God, we desire to honor Him in every detail. As believers, we should ask ourselves if our conscience gets bothered by little things. Remember! There's no such thing as a small step on the road to temptation or on the pathway to revenge or retaliation.

1 Samuel 25

"When the LORD deals well with my lord, then remember your maid-servant." —*1 Samuel 25.31*

After he dishonored David, Nabal's life hung in the balance. What a fool he was! His wife, Abigail, realized that. So she decided to do something to rescue him from sure death. She thought, *Perhaps a lot of food and a pleading message from me will turn David's heart.* Abigail had already considered what she was going to do and say to save her husband's life. First, she fell on her face before David. Then, she expressed her faith in God's good plan for David. We can be certain that along the way she prayed fervently for God to intervene. Often when we are faced with a crisis, our standard, garden-variety answer is to sort of tuck our tails between our legs, run into a corner, and let cobwebs form on us. But there is a better way to find a solution. It takes creativity, determination, and trust in the Lord. And when He pulls it off, it's marvelous.

1 Samuel 26

Then Saul said, "I have sinned. Return, my son David, for I will not harm you again because my life was precious in your sight this day. Behold, I have played the fool and have committed a serious error." —*1 Samuel 26:21*

Saul's life (not unlike Nabal's) can be summed up in one word: foolish. He was a king who could have been David's role model and mentor, but instead he almost became David's murderer. He willfully disobeyed God and "played the fool" (1 Samuel 26:21). But Saul not only lived a foolish life, he eventually died a tragic death. When Philistine arrows pierced his body, Saul told his armor bearer to draw his sword and finish Saul off (31:4) He did not want to suffer the indignity of having the Philistines mock him in death. He was concerned about his image with the enemy but showed little concern for his relationship with God whom he was about to meet. Believers can also live foolish lives and reap tragic consequences. That happens when disobedience dulls our senses. We get very concerned with what people think, and we lose contact with what God thinks. Ultimately, only the Lord's opinion matters.

1 Samuel 27

Then David said to himself, "Now I will perish one day by the hand of Saul. There is nothing better for me than to escape into the land of the Philistines. Saul then will despair of searching for me anymore in all the territory of Israel, and I will escape from his hand."

—1 Samuel 27:1

David should have known better. Samuel had anointed him with oil and assured him he would one day be the king. But David ignored God's promise and chose pessimism. He thought, *God has deserted me. Now I'll never be king. I'm gonna die if I keep on the front edge of Saul's army. They'll finally catch up with me. I have to escape. The best solution is to go to Philistia.* What a picture of a Christian who deliberately opts for carnality over spirituality.

David, at this point in his life, was a believer on the inside, but he looked like a nonbeliever on the outside. Christians should not follow the example of David at this point in his life when he chose to hide with his enemy, to disobey God, and to operate in the flesh. When the future seems bleak, believers in Christ should put our faith in God and hold firmly to His promises.

1 Samuel 28

Then Saul said to his servants, "Seek for me a woman who is a medium, that I may go to her and inquire of her." And his servants said to him, "Behold, there is a woman who is a medium at En-dor."
—1 Samuel 28:7

The Bible tells of a man who sought to know the future because he was scared to death of the present. He was a king. He sought wisdom from a "spiritist," a medium, who lived in a city named Endor. When Saul went through the process of calling up Samuel from the dead and listening to his voice, it was a terrible, frightening experience, which led ultimately to the death of King Saul (1 Chronicles 10:13). Saul's disobedience had a simple beginning, perhaps prompted only by curiosity and fantasy, but it led to a tragic ending. As Christians, how should we respond to a culture that is fascinated by magic? There's a very fine line between fun games and black magic. This stuff is not child's play. Believers must get rid of all the related books or trinkets or horoscopes or omens in tangible form. Accessing them is demonic, and it has serious spiritual consequences. It's best to burn them.

1 Samuel 29

Achish said to the commanders of the Philistines, "Is this not David, the servant of Saul the king of Israel, who has been with me these days, or rather these years?" —1 Samuel 29:3

Slumping into despondency can lead us downward. We may think, *Oh, it won't hurt. What's a couple of months of carnality compared to a lifetime of obedience?* It doesn't work like that. The downward pull into the abyss of sin is subtle and deadly. When David went to Philistia to hide from Saul, he ended up staying for *sixteen months*. This was the man known as "the sweet psalmist of Israel" (2 Samuel 23:1). Yet there's not one psalm attributed to those days when he was with Achish in Gath and Ziklag. Of course not! He couldn't sing the Lord's song in a foreign land governed by the enemy's influence! When believers slump into a depression as a result of prolonged sin, joy does not flow from their hearts, words, or lives. When we find ourselves there, how much better to turn to the Lord, receive His forgiveness, and seek help for climbing out of the pit.

1 Samuel 30

Moreover David was greatly distressed because the people spoke of stoning him, for all the people were embittered, each one because of his sons and his daughters. But David strengthened himself in the Lord his God. —1 Samuel 30:6

How does anyone press on when the bottom drops out? A very helpful principle emerges from the life of David as he found himself unable to escape those tough times. As he and his fellow warriors were returning from battle, they came upon a scene that took their breath away. What had once been their own quiet village was now a black heap of smoldering ruins. To make matters worse, their wives and children had been kidnapped. And if that were not bad enough, David's own men turned against him. If ever a man felt like hanging it up, David did. But he didn't hang it up. Instead, "David strengthened himself in the LORD his God" (1 Samuel 30:6). Christians can learn from David's example. We can pour out our hearts to the Lord and remember that God is "a very present help" (Psalm 46:1). Once we get things squared away vertically, it will help clear away the fog horizontally.

1 Samuel 31

They put his weapons in the temple of Ashtaroth, and they fastened his body to the wall of Beth-shan.   *—1 Samuel 31:10*

Saul, the king who once knew the joys and blessings of the kingdom, the man who was the representative of God to the chosen people, the man who cared so much about his image, was now dead. His lifeless body was mutilated, and his severed head was carried and put on display from place to place. The Philistines made light of his death and, no doubt, made profane comments about Jehovah, the God of Saul and the Israelites. What a horrible, tragic scene! The greatest tragedy of all was that this man need not have died like this. But the truth is he chose his path. This is what happens when Christians inch out compromise or disobedience in our lives, one day after another, nullifying our testimony, eroding into mediocrity, living like the lost world. In contrast, Christ calls us to be different . . . to take up our cross daily and to follow Him in obedience.

Second Samuel

2 Samuel 1

*Then David chanted with this lament over Saul and Jonathan
his son.*   *—2 Samuel 1:17*

For the first fifty years of his life, David walked in the integrity of
his heart and God granted him success. Though there were a few
temporary excursions into sin, most of David's young adult years
were years of triumph. Because of David's many mighty acts, it
is easy to forget that for a dozen or more years he lived as a fugitive and spent many hours of disillusionment in the wilderness,
hiding from a murderous King Saul. But it was in the afflictions
that David learned how to lead . . . especially while he was a cave
dweller. Eventually, he became king, the second king of Israel,
chosen and anointed by God Himself. But with his adversary,
Saul, dead, David didn't cheer; he mourned. When God deals
harshly with someone we don't like, do we rejoice or grieve?
Every human life is sacred in God's eyes. Christians should value
the lives of friends and foes alike.

2 Samuel 2

*Then it came about afterwards that David inquired of the LORD, say-
ing, "Shall I go up to one of the cities of Judah?" And the LORD said
to him, "Go up." So David said, "Where shall I go up?" And He said,
"To Hebron."*   *—2 Samuel 2:1*

David remembered when Samuel anointed him and whispered,
"You will be the next king," so David asked the Lord, "Shall I
go up to one of the cities?" (2 Samuel 2:1). He really wanted
to know, "Is it time now, Lord?" He didn't march into Israel to

take over the whole nation. He waited patiently on God for further instruction. And God revealed His plan to David. He said, in effect, "Begin your reign in Hebron." In those days, the Lord spoke audibly, but today He speaks from His Word. Today, we may find ourselves in situations in which we wonder, "God has obviously opened the door, and I'm about to walk through it. But . . . is that what I should do?" Our tendency is to race in when there is some benefit, some strategic opportunity, that will come our way. Sometimes it's best to begin very quietly . . . to apply restraint . . . to pace our first steps with great care.

2 Samuel 3

Sons were born to David at Hebron: his firstborn was Amnon, by Ahinoam the Jezreelitess; and his second, Chileab, by Abigail the widow of Nabal the Carmelite; and the third, Absalom the son of Maacah, the daughter of Talmai, king of Geshur . . . and the sixth, Ithream, by David's wife Eglah. —2 Samuel 3:2–5

This seemingly uninteresting genealogy tells us something about the weak side of David's character. David didn't simply have six children . . . he had six children by six different wives. He also had, along with the wives, some of whom aren't mentioned here, a number of nameless concubines. Polygamy was one of the dark spots in David's life that later came back to haunt him. Being a man of virility, he gave himself passionately to these women; the result was too many children who were thrown together to raise themselves. David had too many wives and too many children to lead and rear properly. Christians today probably don't struggle with an oversized family, but we may lead lives that are overly busy—too busy to invest enough time in our spouse and our children. By giving insufficient parental direction and guidance, even Christian parents can rear undisciplined children and produce prodigals.

2 Samuel 4

Now Jonathan, Saul's son, had a son crippled in his feet. He was five years old when the report of Saul and Jonathan came from Jezreel, and his nurse took him up and fled. And it happened that in her hurry to flee, he fell and became lame. And his name was Mephibosheth. —2 Samuel 4:4

It was the custom in eastern dynasties that when a new king took over, all the family members of the previous dynasty were exterminated to take away the possibility of revolt. So Jonathan asked David to spare his life when David came to the throne (1 Samuel 20:13–14). Without hesitation, David agreed and entered into a binding covenant with his friend. When David became king, he asked, "Is there yet anyone left of the house of Saul, that I may show him kindness for Jonathan's sake?" (2 Samuel 9:1). He didn't ask, "Is there anyone qualified or worthy?" but "Is there *anyone*?" And there was. King David showed grace to Jonathan's disabled son, Mephibosheth. Grace isn't picky. Grace doesn't look for things that have been done that earn favor or deserve love. Grace is God giving Himself to someone who does not deserve it and will never be able to repay it. Let's extend this kind of grace to someone today.

2 Samuel 5

*And David realized that the LORD had . . . exalted his kingdom for
the sake of His people Israel. Meanwhile David took more concubines
and wives from Jerusalem, after he came from Hebron; and more
sons and daughters were born to David.* —2 *Samuel 5:12–13*

When King David committed adultery with Bathsheba and had
her husband, Uriah, killed in battle, he didn't fall suddenly. Some
cracks had already begun to show in his spiritual armor. David
was amassing his fortune along with a number of wives. But
when was enough enough? He had a harem-full, and he was still
not satisfied, driven by lust for more. Gross sin isn't a sudden
action; it's the result of multiple bad choices. The only hope we
have is daily dependence on the living Lord. It's the only way we
can make it. He's touched by our feelings of infirmity, our weaknesses . . . our inability in the dark and lonely times to say no.
And God says, "I'm ready with all the power you need. Call on
Me and I will give you what you need." So? Call on Him! Stop
this moment and call on Him. He will hear and heed the prayers
of His children.

2 Samuel 6

*So they brought it with the ark of God from the house of Abinadab,
which was on the hill; and Ahio was walking ahead of the ark.*
—2 Samuel 6:4

When David took the throne as king, he realized that the ark
of the covenant was not in the city of David . . . therefore, there
was no central place of worship. As a result, the spiritual walk of
the people of Israel had become lukewarm. Their heart was no

longer hot after God. As their leader, David knew that he needed to return that piece of sacred furniture to its rightful place. He needed to set it up as God designed it. God had promised that He would meet with His people above the ark's mercy seat (Exodus 25:22). To Christians, all this sounds so strange. Prior to Calvary, however, so many things of God were found in symbols and types and pictures. But today, God has met with us through the incarnation of Jesus Christ, our risen Lord, and dwells forever in the hearts of His people though His Spirit.

2 Samuel 7

"Go and say to My servant David, 'Thus says the LORD, "Are you the one who should build Me a house to dwell in?"'" —2 Samuel 7:5

Being a man of war—in fact, a very courageous warrior—David was often involved in battle and intensely stressful situations. However, there came an interlude of calm and quiet in his life. David had domestic peace and national rest. And inside his lovely cedar-lined home, as David began to reflect upon the peaceful time, he started to dream. David wanted to build a temple for God. But it wasn't God's plan for David to build a temple. It was a great idea, a great plan in David's heart . . . but it wasn't God's plan. God's response was not God's judgment coming upon David as a consequence of wrong. When God says no, it is not necessarily discipline or rejection. It may simply be redirection. But Christians today struggle with accepting God's no and living with the mystery of His will. Let's learn to trust God's plans instead of our own, even when we don't understand.

2 Samuel 8

And Joram brought with him articles of silver, of gold and of bronze.
King David also dedicated these to the LORD, with the silver and gold
that he had dedicated from all the nations which he had subdued.

—2 Samuel 8:10 11

Under David's reign, the flag over Israel flew with dignity and
honor and respect. Other nations looked on the people of Israel
and said, "Stay away from them. They've got a leader now." The
zealots came out from under the rocks as people began to love
their country. A marked sense of patriotism returned. King David
was a courageous leader with a tender heart toward God. When
God granted him success, David didn't use it to pat himself on
the back or to show the people how great he was. His desire was
to show them how great God was. All the spoils of war David
dedicated to the One who fought for Israel. Christians who desire
to lead others well need only to look to David's example. We
acknowledge that all our successes, good ideas, creativity, and
shrewd management come from God. It is by His power alone
that we are made great and given strength (1 Chronicles 29:12).
That perspective keeps us grateful, keeps us humble.

2 Samuel 9

David said to him, "Do not fear, for I will surely show kindness to
you for the sake of your father Jonathan, and will restore to you all
the land of your grandfather Saul; and you shall eat at my table
regularly."

—2 Samuel 9.7

Imagine what Mephibosheth must have felt at this moment.
Expecting a sword to strike his neck, he heard these unbelievable

words from King David, "You shall eat at my table regularly." Picture what life would be like in the years to come at the supper table with David. The meal is fixed and the dinner bell rings and along come the members of the family and their guests. Then here comes Mephibosheth, King Saul's grandson. He smiles, looks down, and humbly takes his place at the table. David adopted Mephibosheth into his family, and he became one of the king's sons. This is what God does for every sinner who places his or her faith in Jesus—God adopts us into the family of the heavenly King. God has taken us from where we were and brought us to a place of fellowship with Him. Let's thank God for His grace!

2 Samuel 10

When they told it to David, he sent to meet them, for the men were greatly humiliated. And the king said, "Stay at Jericho until your beards grow, and then return." —2 Samuel 10:5

When King David heard about the death of his friend, King Nahash of Ammon, David sent his servants to console Hanun, King Nahash's son. But Hanun took King David's actions as a threat, so he sent David a message—no one would take advantage of Hanun during his time of mourning. Hanun shamed King David's servants by shaving their beards and sending them home half naked. King David respected his men, so he told them to stay in Jericho until their beards grew back and they regained their dignity. While David's men faced temporary shame, those who die without having received forgiveness through Jesus Christ will experience permanent shame. And even believers in Christ feel appropriate shame when they fall into sin. But thankfully, Jesus

Christ faced the cross, scorning its shame, and won the victory over sin (Hebrews 12:2). Grace awaits believers and unbelievers who carry the burden of shame to Christ.

2 Samuel 11

Then it happened in the spring, at the time when kings go out to battle, that David sent Joab and his servants with him and all Israel, and they destroyed the sons of Ammon and besieged Rabbah. But David stayed at Jerusalem. —2 Samuel 11:1

Fresh off a series of victories on the battlefield, David was at an all-time high. He had ample money, incredible power, unquestioned authority, and remarkable fame. Therefore, he was vulnerable. Perhaps he became a tad impressed by his own track record because in 2 Samuel 11:1, David indulged himself. David was in bed, not in battle. Had he been where he belonged — with his troops — the Bathsheba episode would never have been. Our greatest battles don't usually come when we're working hard; they come when we have too much unguarded leisure. Hard times create dependent people. We don't become proud when we're dependent on God. Survival keeps believers humble. Pride happens when everything is swinging in our direction. When we are growing in prestige and fame and significance, that's the time to watch out! In good times and struggles, we Christians should evaluate our thoughts and examine our lives according to Scripture . . . and, of course, surround ourselves with accountability.

2 Samuel 12

Then David's anger burned greatly against the man, and he said to Nathan, "As the Lord lives, surely the man who has done this deserves to die." . . . Nathan then said to David, "You are the man!"
—*2 Samuel 12:5, 7*

David wasn't relaxing, taking life easy, and sipping lemonade on his patio during the aftermath of his adultery. For months on end, he had sleepless nights. He had no joy. Then the prophet Nathan stepped in and told David the truth. As a result of the wise words of Nathan, David was in a most vulnerable spot. Moved with compassion over the story of the poor man and his stolen sheep, David acknowledged his sin and repented. It was an incredible confrontation. Not all confrontations end like Nathan's did with David. Sometimes there is no repentance. The work of confrontation is the most severe work of the Holy Spirit. Either we are keeping short accounts with our heavenly Father as His child or we are living a lie. When we repent, God promises us restitution and forgiveness through the blood of Jesus Christ. While He does not promise relief from any and all consequences, He promises peace that only the Spirit of God can give.

2 Samuel 13

Now when King David heard of all these matters, he was very angry.
—*2 Samuel 13:21*

What kind of palace did David provide for his umpteen wives and children? On the surface, it was fabulous. They probably had every material thing they wanted. But money cannot buy the best things in life, and possessions can't solve problems within relationships at home. This was true in David's palace too. For example, Amnon was attracted to his half-sister, Tamar, the blood sister of Absalom. It was a disgraceful, disgusting kind of attraction. Better defined, it was incestuous lust. With the help of a friend, Amnon set up a scenario that brought Tamar into his presence, and he raped her. Where was their father during all this? Absent! If we as believers have fallen into the trap of passivity and preoccupation with material things and have neglected the relationships in our lives, we should turn around now. Broken and bruised, let's just lay it all out before God and ask Him for the grace and strength to face the consequences straight on and begin doing what is right.

2 Samuel 14

Therefore he said to his servants, "See, Joab's field is next to mine, and he has barley there; go and set it on fire." So Absalom's servants set the field on fire. —2 Samuel 14:30

Remember Absalom, the young man who never learned responsibility? After killing his brother, Amnon, for raping Tamar, Absalom fled. David invited him back to Jerusalem but made him live in his own house, separate from David. Seething with resentment over his father's refusal to see him, Absalom went to the extreme. He burned the crops of Joab, David's friend, in order to get his father's attention. Absalom never forgot the wounds King David had inflicted while Absalom was in his adolescent years—when David neglected to punish Amnon for raping Tamar. Adolescence is a challenging period, not only for the young but also, especially, for the parents. In order to survive this period, Christian parents must stay open and flexible and be willing to learn as much as they teach during these growing-up years. Adolescents begin to ask hard questions. The more rigid parents are, the less their children ask . . . and the more wrong opinions the children form on their own or from the street.

2 Samuel 15

Now behold, Zadok also came, and all the Levites with him carrying the ark of the covenant of God. And they set down the ark of God, and Abiathar came up until all the people had finished passing from the city.　　　　　　　　　　　*—2 Samuel 15:24*

After David's son Absalom betrayed him and tried to usurp the throne, David took the ark of the covenant and fled. More than ever, David needed a friend. Zadok and Abiathar were friends who stood by to shelter David. These two men were Levites, and they came alongside David, carrying the ark of the covenant. They set that heavy, sacred chest down, looked over at David, and said, "We're with you, David. We've been with you all along." "Take the ark back to the city," David told his buddies. Out of respect, that's exactly what they did. They were there to help David, regardless. We all need Zadoks and Abiathars in our lives. Friends are not optional; they're essential. There is no substitute for a loyal friend—someone to care, to listen, to comfort, and yes, occasionally to reprove. Believers in Christ should invest time and effort to cultivate deep friendships.

2 Samuel 16

So they pitched a tent for Absalom on the roof, and Absalom went in to his father's concubines in the sight of all Israel. —2 Samuel 16:22

There are two kinds of trouble a family can experience: trouble from without and trouble from within. Trouble from within devastated David's household. David had been forgiven of his sin with Bathsheba, but he had to live with its ongoing consequences. God had pronounced that one of David's "companions" would lie with David's wives in broad daylight (2 Samuel 12:11). The Hebrew word for "companion" is an intimate term most likely referring to one of David's own children. In fact, that is exactly what happened years after David's adulterous affair. His own son, Absalom, had relations with some of David's concubines. Though God graciously forgives Christians, we often tell ourselves that grace means that all consequences for sin are removed. Sometimes that mentality allows us to be sucked under by the power of the flesh. But we have the power in the person of the Holy Spirit to say no to sin at every turn in our lives.

2 Samuel 17

Now when David had come to Mahanaim, Shobi . . . Machir . . . and Barzillai . . . brought beds, basins, pottery, wheat, barley, flour, parched grain, beans, lentils, parched seeds . . . for they said, "The people are hungry and weary and thirsty in the wilderness."
—2 Samuel 17:27–29

Without realizing it, we have been trained to think that the most significant people are star athletes, actors, and musicians. But most often, the people worth noting are the individuals who give selflessly for the benefit of another and never receive any credit. A group of friends who sheltered David were Shobi, Machir, and Barzillai. And as a result, these nobodies became a group of somebodies in David's corner. Their lives were important, even though they weren't well-known. As Christians, we should pursue significance instead of renown. People of significance share common traits. They have a selfless devotion. High-impact people don't care who gets the credit, and they never complain about the roles they fill. They have a mission focus — they focus on the right objectives, and they don't waste their time pursuing things that don't matter. And they have a contagious joy that inspires humility and unity. Let's commit to pursuing godly rather than worldly significance.

2 Samuel 18

The king charged Joab and Abishai and Ittai, saying, "Deal gently for my sake with the young man Absalom." And all the people heard when the king charged all the commanders concerning Absalom.
— 2 Samuel 18:5

Born into David's home was a young man with a rebel heart — Absalom. Absalom had been wounded by his father's neglect. David was too busy with the things of the kingdom. But when Absalom led an insurrection against the throne, David finally had to deal with Absalom's rebellion. So the king organized his forces into three groups under three commanders and ordered all three men to "deal gently for my sake with the young man Absalom" (2 Samuel 18:5). Those were David's clear instructions. That day David's army defeated Israel's army, killing twenty thousand men, including his son Absalom. King David's pain was borderline unbearable. David loved Absalom no matter how wicked his actions were. The king's love for his wayward son gives us a small glimpse into God's love for us. When we consider how much God's grace outweighs our sin, it can help us to extend mercy to those who have hurt us.

2 Samuel 19

The king said to Shimei, "You shall not die." Thus the king swore to him. —2 Samuel 19:23

When on the run from his son Absalom, who had usurped the throne, David was at his lowest ebb. Then a man named Shimei, part of Saul's family, came out of nowhere, cursed David, and hurled rocks at him (2 Samuel 16.5–13). Fast forward to after Absalom's death. David passed by Shimei's town again on his way back to his throne. This time Shimei begged for forgiveness. Though Shimei deserved death, David forgave him. How could he do that? First, his vertical focus never got out of sync. And secondly, David was very much aware of his own failure. The forgiven make good "forgivers." To forgive another, we must recall times in our lives when we needed forgiveness. And we must verbalize our forgiveness: "I forgive you. Let's start over." Through Jesus Christ, God has forgiven believers and given us a new beginning when we deserved just the opposite.

2 Samuel 20

So all the men of Israel withdrew from following David and followed Sheba the son of Bichri; but the men of Judah remained steadfast to their king, from the Jordan even to Jerusalem. —2 Samuel 20:2

One of the characteristics of our fallen nature is rebellion. That is true today, and it was true in biblical times. While King David traveled to Jerusalem, the people of Israel and the people of Judah refused to get along. Finally, Sheba, a troublemaker, incited the people of Israel to abandon God's anointed king and follow him instead. Sheba led others in defying the Lord. What does God think about rebellion? Deuteronomy 21:18–21 tells us how God dealt with it in the days of the Law—defiant young men were to be killed. God does not wink at defiance. So how can we as Christians prevent rebellion in our lives? Defiance begins with carnal attitudes, when we say, "I want *my* own way, not God's way! And I won't quit until I get it." When believers start thinking this way, we should stop, drop to our knees, and seek God's forgiveness.

2 Samuel 21

Now when the Philistines were at war again with Israel, David went down and his servants with him; and as they fought against the Philistines, David became weary. —2 Samuel 21:15

David suffered the anguish and grief of the premature death of his son Absalom, who was murdered following the conspiracy he led against his father. Another blow that drove David to his knees was a three-year famine that struck the land, adding calamity to humiliation. And finally, the nation was back at war with its age-old enemy, the Philistines. And as he fought the Philistines, David hit a wall of physical, spiritual, and emotional exhaustion. After all he'd been through, who wouldn't feel exhausted? But some wise counselors encouraged David to stay home from battle—to rest. He needed a break! Like David, Christians can remember that when our fast-paced lives wear us down, the Lord gives us rest (Matthew 11:28). Rest is not for the weak—it's for those who recognize that their strength and endurance ultimately come from God. So when life's battles exhaust us, let's slow down and refresh our souls in the Lord.

2 Samuel 22

"For You are my lamp, O LORD, / And the LORD illumines my darkness." —2 Samuel 22:29

When exhaustion hit David like a ton of bricks, he lifted his hands to God and declared his feelings in a song. But the tone was not what one might expect, given his circumstances. It was not a dark, somber dirge, but a psalm of praise that the gifted, aging composer sang to the Lord (2 Samuel 22:1). David summed up his faith in four themes, four expressions that threaded their way through his psalm of praise. Like David, believers face seasons of struggle and fatigue. We can remember these four truths when those times come. First, when times are tough, God is our only security. Second, when our days are dark, the Lord is our only light. Third, when our walk is weak, the Lord is our only strength. And fourth, when our future is uncertain, the Lord is our only hope. He is our light and our salvation; whom should we fear?

2 Samuel 23

"Truly is not my house so with God?
For He has made an everlasting covenant with me,
Ordered in all things, and secured;
For all my salvation and all my desire,
Will He not indeed make it grow?"　　　　　*—2 Samuel 23:5*

The long shadows of age and pressure fell across David's face. He had lived a full life, experienced both the heights and the depths, and finally entered the twilight years. David often had to trust God in impossible circumstances. And the king's final words sum up the lessons he learned. As he struggled, David learned that God was no distant Deity, preoccupied with other galaxies or concerned with the changing of the seasons. David's God heard his voice and responded to his cries with grace. As believers, when times are tough, we have no trouble believing the truth about calamity and distress and death. But at those times, it is so difficult to believe that the Lord delights in us. Yet He does. That's the whole message of grace. The Lord dispatches His angels of hope who bring invincible help because He delights in us. He cares for us! Thank God for His abundant grace!

2 Samuel 24

Now David's heart troubled him after he had numbered the people.
So David said to the LORD, "I have sinned greatly in what I have
done. But now, O LORD, please take away the iniquity of Your ser-
vant, for I have acted very foolishly."　　　　　*—2 Samuel 24:10*

Age alone is no guarantee of maturity. When a spiritual leader at any age wanders from the things of God, the consequences are often devastating and always far-reaching. Second Samuel 24 portrays a tragic example of this when David, in the later years of his life, committed a sin that resulted in the death of seventy thousand men (2 Samuel 24:15). Following a victorious battle against the Philistines, David was vulnerable. That's when Satan nudged David in his private thoughts and said, in effect, "Why don't you number these people? Let's see how big your kingdom has become" (1 Chronicles 21:1). But after his sinful decision, "David's heart troubled him" (2 Samuel 24:10), and he immediately repented. That's one of the many reasons David was a man after God's heart. Believers should remember that to deny sin's consequences is to reject God's truth. But if we genuinely seek His forgiveness, God will give us grace to endure the consequences.

First Kings

1 Kings 1

His father had never crossed him at any time by asking, "Why have you done so?" And he was also a very handsome man, and he was born after Absalom. —1 Kings 1:6

King David wholeheartedly followed the Lord and loved His Law. So how could David's son Adonijah disobey by trying to usurp the throne? Unfortunately, Adonijah never learned to honor God because King David had never *crossed* his son. From his earliest days, Adonijah had the freedom to do as he pleased. David loved the Lord, followed His commands, and confessed when he disobeyed. But David never disciplined Adonijah as God had disciplined David. So Adonijah didn't learn that his heavenly Father chastens His children because He loves them. Like God, human parents should establish firm boundaries so that kids will learn to exercise their freedom within the limits of God's commands. Even if we model God's parenting of us, there is no guarantee that our kids will never rebel or jump over the boundary fence. God only asks for parents to be faithful to Him. He will take care of the results.

1 Kings 2

"Keep the charge of the LORD your God, to walk in His ways, to keep His statutes, His commandments, His ordinances, and His testimonies, according to what is written in the Law of Moses, that you may succeed in all that you do and wherever you turn." —1 Kings 2:3

Final words reveal what people truly value. With their last few breaths, they have one more chance to share what an entire lifetime has taught them. With his last words, King David exhorted his son Solomon to obey God's Law and seek His blessing. As the leader of the Lord's chosen people, the king served as God's representative, to lead the Israelites in obedience to the Mosaic Law. In order to drive His Word deep into their hearts, God commanded each king to copy His entire Law by hand (Deuteronomy 17:18). This practice taught King David to love God and obey His Word through the struggles and victories of life. And David passed that lesson on to Solomon. What do our lives tell others about God? Remember: our kids, our friends, even our foes watch our actions and listen to our words, because our actions and words reveal whether we truly love God and honor His Word.

1 Kings 3

Now Solomon loved the LORD, walking in the statutes of his father David, except he sacrificed and burned incense on the high places.
— 1 Kings 3:3

King Solomon followed his father's example and obeyed God's Law, except in one area. The Lord had commanded His people to worship Him in one designated place only (Deuteronomy 12:5–6). But King Solomon sacrificed his bulls, goats, and incense in places that God had not authorized. Solomon got lazy when it came to proper worship. While the nations surrounding Israel bowed to their false gods on mountains, under trees, or any other convenient place, God commanded His people to worship Him at the tabernacle (later, at the temple). God required His people to worship on His terms, not theirs. And thousands of years later, this is still true. The Bible instructs Christians to worship God together, as the church, Christ's body. Just as King Solomon disobeyed when he sacrificed to God in the wrong place, we disobey Him if we consistently worship alone, at home, on Sunday mornings (Hebrews 10:23–25).

1 Kings 4

He spoke of trees, from the cedar that is in Lebanon even to the hyssop that grows on the wall; he spoke also of animals and birds and creeping things and fish. —1 Kings 4:33

When he asked for wisdom to rule God's people, King Solomon probably didn't think his understanding would extend to botany, zoology, ornithology, and ichthyology. But the Lord had a purpose in giving Solomon such a vast array of knowledge. God had established Israel in order to draw other nations to Himself. The Lord gave King Solomon great knowledge in order to set him apart as God's chosen leader and to attract kings to His land through Solomon's good reputation. God used King Solomon's wisdom to show other national leaders that the Lord alone is the Creator of all things and the spring of all knowledge. As believers seek understanding in their fields of work, God will give them the insight they need. And as Christians pursue excellence in their lines of work and give God the credit for success, their lives will draw others to the Lord. And He will get the glory.

1 Kings 5

The LORD gave wisdom to Solomon, just as He promised him; and there was peace between Hiram and Solomon, and the two of them made a covenant. —1 Kings 5:12

Just as a little boy doesn't know how to care for himself, Solomon lacked the wisdom he needed to govern God's people. So the king humbled himself before the Lord and asked for wisdom to accomplish his God-ordained task. And in 1 Kings 5:12, God fulfilled His promise to equip King Solomon with supernatural knowledge. As King Solomon planned to build the temple, he recognized the superior ability of the Sidonians to prepare wood, so he made an agreement with Hiram king of Tyre to pay his laborers to provide cedar and cypress wood for temple construction. God gave Solomon wisdom to tackle the difficult task of building God's house. As Christians face obstacles, we can ask God for wisdom and trust that He will come through. No human being can handle the curve balls of life without divine help. God always gives understanding to those who ask in faith (James 1:5).

1 Kings 6

The house, while it was being built, was built of stone prepared at the quarry, and there was neither hammer nor axe nor any iron tool heard in the house while it was being built. —1 Kings 6:7

The sound of hammers, saws, and clanging metal didn't ring from the temple. It was a quiet construction site. Solomon had commanded the laborers to prepare at the quarry the stones for the temple's foundation, walls, and pillars. Then the men lugged the prepared stones to the building site and fitted them together, without metal tools. Solomon organized the construction process in such a way as to maintain a solemn, worshipful environment. Like Solomon, Christians should create an environment conducive to worship. Whether we spend time with the Lord in the morning, afternoon, or the evening, do we take time to remove distractions? If King Solomon could turn a construction site into a place of worship, we can turn off the TV, put away our smartphones, and choose to worship God in quiet reverence. Our Lord deserves our undivided focus and wholehearted devotion.

1 Kings 7

Now Solomon was building his own house thirteen years, and he finished all his house. —*1 Kings 7:1*

Enter through ornately carved doors to the living areas paneled with expensive cedar. Pass by towering bronze pillars. Walk on shiny marble floors. This beautiful decor describes King Solomon's palace. It took thirteen years for the workers to finish Solomon's palace complex, which included multiple buildings, but it took only seven years to build God's temple. The majesty of Solomon's house recalls God's promise not only to give the king wisdom but also to bless him with wealth. God rewarded King Solomon for his humility and his desire to govern the Israelites well. And when we as believers strive to honor the Lord in every aspect of our lives, God will bless us—not necessarily with money and fame but with eternal, heavenly reward. And as we humbly depend on Him, the Lord will fulfill His promise to equip us in all our endeavors.

1 Kings 8

It happened that when the priests came from the holy place, the cloud filled the house of the LORD, so that the priests could not stand to minister because of the cloud, for the glory of the LORD filled the house of the LORD. —*1 Kings 8:10–11*

After the priests installed the ark behind the veil, the glory of the Lord permeated the temple. A thick fog enveloped the priests so that they couldn't see their hands in front of their faces. While fear may have gripped their hearts, the cloud revealed God's dwelling among His people. Because the Lord is spirit, He revealed

His glory in the form of a dark cloud. When Moses ascended the mountain to commune with God, he entered a thick fog. In the tabernacle, within the holy of holies, God's presence rested in a cloud over the mercy seat. And after the priests placed the ark in the most holy place, God inhabited His newly built temple. Today, the Lord doesn't live in a physical building, nor does He reveal His presence in a dark cloud. God dwells among His people, the church, as the Holy Spirit takes up residence in each believer's life.

1 Kings 9

"Then I will establish the throne of your kingdom over Israel forever, just as I promised to your father David, saying, 'You shall not lack a man on the throne of Israel.'"   —1 Kings 9:5

God made a covenant with King David and promised that one of his descendants would always rule over Israel. When King Solomon came to power, the Lord reminded him of His promise. But He also warned Solomon and all of Israel not to engage in idolatry or God would bring judgment upon them. Unfortunately, King Solomon, along with his foreign wives, burned incense and worshiped idols. The Lord disciplined King Solomon by eventually dividing the kingdom, but God still established Solomon's son as king over Judah. Even when Solomon turned away from God, God graciously kept His covenant with King David. The Lord always keeps His promises. He remains faithful even when we break faith. Though at times we fail Him and dishonor His name, God will never reject the children He has adopted through Jesus Christ. God's faithful character isn't a license to sin, however. Rather, His grace draws us to repentance.

1 Kings 10

Now Solomon gathered chariots and horsemen; and he had 1,400 chariots and 12,000 horsemen, and he stationed them in the chariot cities and with the king in Jerusalem. — 1 Kings 10:26

What's wrong with a few chariots and horsemen? King Solomon built his military and equipped it with the best weapons money could buy. He imported expensive chariots and horses from Egypt. A wise ruler strives to assemble a massive army to protect innocent civilians from enemies. Unless, of course, the Lord says not to. Solomon must have forgotten about Deuteronomy 17:16 in which the Lord commanded the kings of Israel not to build large armies and not to purchase armaments from Egypt. God wanted His people to depend on Him for protection, not on horses and chariots from Egypt — the land from which the Lord had rescued them. God still expects His people to trust in Him instead of in the things they formerly depended on, such as jobs, money, and relationships. Christians must plan for the future. But wisdom demands that we trust ultimately in the Lord to protect and provide for us.

1 Kings 11

For when Solomon was old, his wives turned his heart away after other gods; and his heart was not wholly devoted to the LORD his God, as the heart of David his father had been. — 1 Kings 11:4

Just as a guardrail protects drivers from veering off a mountain road into a ravine, God's commandments protect His children from moral destruction. In Deuteronomy 7:3 – 4, God established a wall of protection around Hebrew marriages. He prohibited the Israelites from marrying foreigners, lest they lead His people toward idolatry. Unfortunately, King Solomon smashed through God's guardrail and plummeted into the chasm of idol worship. But God showed Solomon grace. The Lord promised to punish King Solomon by tearing part of the kingdom from David's descendants and splitting Israel into two nations. But He didn't do it until after Solomon's death. God still sets up barricades to protect His children. His Word prohibits certain actions, not because God is a cosmic killjoy, but because He loves us. Yet, even when we crash through God's boundary fences, He responds with grace. Consequences will come, but God forgives.

1 Kings 12

But he forsook the counsel of the elders which they had given him, and consulted with the young men who grew up with him and served him. —1 Kings 12:8

Throughout Israel's history, certain men who gained a reputation for the wise application of God's Law served as elders. The elders played a role in governing at the local and national levels. So when King Rehoboam's subjects asked him for lower taxes and less forced labor, he went to the elders for guidance. But when the elders told Rehoboam to lighten the peoples' burden, the king refused. King Rehoboam didn't want to diminish his power by following the elders' guidance. So he forsook the elders and sought the counsel of his peers, because he knew they would support his desire to continue oppressing God's people. Like Rehoboam, we tend to seek those who will tell us what we want to hear. When Christians face difficult decisions, we shouldn't ask only our friends what to do. First, we must appeal to God for wisdom. Then we must ask for *and follow* the guidance of godly men and women who demonstrate mature faith.

1 Kings 13

The king said to the man of God, "Please entreat the LORD your God, and pray for me, that my hand may be restored to me." So the man of God entreated the LORD, and the king's hand was restored to him, and it became as it was before.   — 1 Kings 13:6

God doesn't reserve His grace just for believers. Often, He answers the desperate prayers of nonbelievers too. Jeroboam, the king of Israel, feared that if his citizens traveled to Jerusalem to worship God, they would desert him and serve Rehoboam king of Judah. So Jeroboam made two golden calves for the people of the northern kingdom to worship. But one day, as Jeroboam burned incense to an idol, the Lord sent a prophet to warn him about God's impending judgment. As Jeroboam reached out his hand to seize the prophet, the Lord caused Jeroboam's hand to wither so that he couldn't move it. Desperate, the king begged the prophet to ask God for healing. Even though Jeroboam was a pagan, God graciously healed him. Thank God that His grace extends even to those who don't yet know Him! Christians should pray that unbelievers would recognize God's grace and turn to Him in faith.

1 Kings 14

"Therefore behold, I am bringing calamity on the house of Jeroboam, and will cut off from Jeroboam every male person, both bond and free in Israel, and I will make a clean sweep of the house of Jeroboam, as one sweeps away dung until it is all gone."   — 1 Kings 14:10

Just as surely as the sun rises and sets, God will one day deal with evil. His justice will not fail, though at times it seems slow. That was true in the life of King Jeroboam. After God selected

Jeroboam as king over the northern kingdom of Israel, Jeroboam forged idols and engaged in pagan rituals. As God's anointed king, Jeroboam didn't expect God to judge him. But the Lord is just. Not only did God punish King Jeroboam for leading the people in evil, the Lord also promised to kill every male member of Jeroboam's family. God's justice eventually swept away Jeroboam's name from the earth. Today, the Lord patiently extends grace to sinners so they can turn to Him in faith. But He won't wait forever. One day Jesus Christ will return and deal with evil and evildoers once and for all. The Lord's justice does not fail.

1 Kings 15

He also removed Maacah his mother from being queen mother, because she had made a horrid image as an Asherah; and Asa cut down her horrid image and burned it at the brook Kidron.
—1 Kings 15:13

Sometimes our families bring us down. Asa, King of Judah, struggled to honor God in the midst of an evil people. But evil hit close to home when Asa's mother, Maacah, made an offensive idol and bowed down to it. Asa had a choice—honor God or honor his mother. Asa chose to honor God by cutting his mom's idol into pieces and burning it. But he didn't stop there. Asa also took away her title, "queen mother," and all the privileges that came with it. King Asa valued God's Law more than he valued Maacah's approval. Asa's actions pleased God. First Kings 15:11 says that King Asa followed the Lord just as his ancestor King David had done. God commands His people to love their families. But at times Christians must distance themselves, especially when their family members' actions consistently and directly contradict God's Word. Our first allegiance is to God.

1 Kings 16

In his days Hiel the Bethelite built Jericho; he laid its foundations
with the loss of Abiram his firstborn, and set up its gates with the loss
of his youngest son Segub, according to the word of the LORD, which
He spoke by Joshua the son of Nun. —1 Kings 16:34

King Ahab worshiped idols and led all of Israel to disobey the
Lord. Instead of demonstrating the fear of the Lord, Ahab created
in Israel an atmosphere of rebellion. Very few people under King
Ahab's rule knew or revered God's Law. In this climate of defiance, Hiel the Bethelite rebuilt Jericho. Hiel either didn't know or
didn't care that after Joshua led the Israelites in the supernatural
defeat of Jericho, the Lord commanded them never to recon-
struct the city. The ruins in Jericho were to remind Israel that
God alone deserved their worship. Hiel probably didn't know
that his punishment for reconstructing Jericho would be the
deaths of his oldest and youngest children (Joshua 6:26). When
we disregard God's Word, it has devastating consequences. The
Lord wants Christians' lives to create an atmosphere of reverence
for His Word. Let's live so that our actions lead others away from
selfishness and toward submission to God's Word.

1 Kings 17

Then Elijah said to her, "Do not fear; go, do as you have said, but
make me a little bread cake from it first and bring it out to me, and
afterward you may make one for yourself and for your son."
—1 Kings 17:13

God withheld the rain, and the parched earth cracked. The
Lord cursed His land because of King Ahab's evil deeds. And the
drought, which lasted several years, caused hunger and poverty

for many people. As Elijah traveled to find food, he met a widow who was preparing the final meal for herself and her son. The widow had no hope of surviving the famine. But Elijah told her not to fear because the Lord had promised to provide for her until the rain returned. When Elijah asked her to split her two meals into three and to give Elijah the first serving, she agreed. The Sidonian widow, a Gentile, trusted in the God of Israel, despite the odds. That same God still promises to provide for His people (Matthew 6:25–33). The widow shared with Elijah out of her poverty because she trusted in God's ability to provide. Do we trust Him enough to step out in faith?

1 Kings 18

It came about at noon, that Elijah mocked them and said, "Call out with a loud voice, for he is a god; either he is occupied or gone aside, or is on a journey, or perhaps he is asleep and needs to be awakened."　　　　　　　　　　　　　　　　　　　—1 Kings 18:27

In one corner: Elijah, the prophet of God. In the other corner: 450 prophets of Baal. Elijah challenged the prophets of Baal to an epic battle in order to prove that Yahweh ruled over heaven and earth. So as the servants of Baal called on their god with a frenzied ritual of dancing and chanting, Elijah sat back and mocked them. "Surely Baal has the power to answer, but he must be out of town or taking a nap!" Elijah knew that a god who isn't capable of answering his people doesn't deserve worship. And Elijah knew that our God does not sleep. He rules over heaven and earth and nothing escapes His notice. God responded to Elijah's prayer and He will respond to ours too. So don't look for guidance from horoscopes, the stock market, or pop culture.

Let's approach His throne of grace with confidence and find help in our time of need.

1 Kings 19

And he was afraid and arose and ran for his life and came to Beersheba, which belongs to Judah, and left his servant there.
—*1 Kings 19:3*

One minute Elijah stood victorious on the mountain top, having proved the superiority of Yahweh over Baal. The next minute Elijah ran for his life and hid from Queen Jezebel. Elijah had just witnessed God's defeat of 450 prophets of Baal, watched God send supernatural fire from heaven, and felt the cold rain on his face for the first time in years. When Jezebel heard about Elijah's actions, which had resulted in the deaths of all the Baal prophets, she threatened to kill Elijah. Instead of trusting in God, Elijah ran. The fact that Elijah's confidence in God quickly gave way to fear shows that often after a spiritual high, we're more susceptible to a spiritual low. When we experience victory over sin or a fruitful ministry to others, we can expect temptation and fear to follow. Let's anticipate the valleys that follow mountain-top experiences and arm ourselves with God's Word and prayer.

1 Kings 20

"About this time tomorrow I will send my servants to you, and they will search your house and the houses of your servants; and whatever is desirable in your eyes, they will take in their hand and carry away."
—*1 Kings 20:6*

Israel and Aram were almost always at war. So when King Ben-Hadad of Aram attacked Samaria and demanded that King Ahab give up his gold, silver, most beautiful wives, and favorite children, Ahab said okay. Rather than praying to God for deliverance, King Ahab gave in to Ben-Hadad's demands. But King Ben-Hadad of Aram wasn't content with taking King Ahab's money and family. When Ben-Hadad came to attack Israel, he wanted to take everything of value to Ahab. King Ben-Hadad's all-consuming greed reminds us of the nature of evil, which destroys everything we value. When Ahab gave in to Ben-Hadad's first request, Ahab opened the floodgates for Ben-Hadad's insatiable hunger. Likewise, when Christians succumb to temptation, it opens the door for more destruction. Satan prowls around like a hungry lion looking to devour Christians. Christians must put on the armor of God, cling to His Word, and fight against the temptation to sin (Ephesians 6:10–17).

1 Kings 21

So Ahab came into his house sullen and vexed because of the word which Naboth the Jezreelite had spoken to him; for he said, "I will not give you the inheritance of my fathers." And he lay down on his bed and turned away his face and ate no food. —1 Kings 21:4

Is there anything more pathetic than a grown man throwing a pity party? That's exactly what King Ahab did when he didn't get what he wanted. From his palace, King Ahab spotted a desirable vineyard. So Ahab tried to buy the vineyard from the owner, Naboth. But when Naboth said no, King Ahab stormed back home, sulked, and refused to eat. Eventually, Jezebel arranged Naboth's murder so that King Ahab would get the vineyard. Ahab personified selfishness. And God hates selfishness. When Christians switch their focus from God's glory to their own desires, they tend to grumble against Him when those desires aren't met. God isn't in the business of giving us everything we want. But He does want to teach His children to put the needs of others before their own. Then Christians will look more like Christ, who came not to be served but to serve others.

1 Kings 22

They washed the chariot by the pool of Samaria, and the dogs licked up his blood . . . according to the word of the LORD which He spoke.
—*1 Kings 22:38*

When we recognize God's sovereign work in our lives, we realize that no event is an accident. After King Ahab murdered Naboth and stole his vineyard, God promised to judge him. The Lord told Ahab that when he died, dogs would lick up his spilled blood in the same place where they licked Naboth's blood. So when an Aramean archer *randomly* shot an arrow that pierced a vulnerable spot in King Ahab's armor, we see God's hand. Not only did God direct the arrow that killed Ahab, he also orchestrated the circumstances following Ahab's death in order to fulfill His promise to Ahab. God caused the king's blood to pool in his chariot, which his servants washed in Samaria, near the vineyard of Naboth. This gory story proves God's sovereign work, not only to exact justice but to fulfill His promises. Since God is at work in our lives, we shouldn't consider any event random.

Second Kings

2 Kings 1

And Ahaziah fell through the lattice in his upper chamber which was in Samaria, and became ill. So he sent messengers and said to them, "Go, inquire of Baal-zebub, the god of Ekron, whether I will recover from this sickness. —2 Kings 1:2

After King Ahaziah came to power over Israel upon the death of his father, the young man suffered misfortune. He had a fall which left him bedridden with life-threatening injuries. Though Ahaziah ruled over God's people, his first impulse led him to call upon the Philistine deity, Baal-zebub. However, God's prophet Elijah intercepted Ahaziah's messengers to the false god. Elijah made clear God's continued presence in Israel, despite the wicked ways of her king. Ahaziah would not survive the effects of his injuries (2 Kings 1:4). We have a tendency to forget God's continual presence with us, especially when we engage in or are surrounded by wickedness. The darkness of evil obscures our vision, leaving us to pursue our own idols and selfish desires. When we do so, the consequences of our sin endanger us, putting us on a path not unlike that of one of Israel's wicked kings.

2 Kings 2

Then the men of the city said to Elisha, "Behold now, the situation of this city is pleasant, as my lord sees; but the water is bad and the land is unfruitful." —2 Kings 2:19

Soon after Elisha witnessed his predecessor, Elijah, spirited away to heaven on a chariot of fire, he arrived in Jericho. The men of the city made Elisha aware of the water's poor quality in their area. Bad water meant poor produce. The men hoped that Elisha would do something for them. The people of Jericho followed Elisha's instructions, brought the prophet salt in a new jar, and watched as Elisha threw the salt into the water. The water was purified, and the land became more fruitful than it had been (2 Kings 2:21). God often uses His servants to bring purity to an impure land. Elisha did so in this passage in a distinctly physical sense, but the principle carries into numerous aspects of our lives. Further, we can make a connection between the purity of the waters and fruitfulness. Our purity produces fruit, even if that fruit takes time to blossom.

2 Kings 3

"But now bring me a minstrel." And it came about, when the minstrel played, that the hand of the LORD came upon him. —*2 Kings 3:15*

To protect their territories, the kings of Israel, Judah, and Edom had united their armies to put down the Moabites. Before going to battle, Jehoshaphat king of Judah called for a prophet of the Lord to advise them on their mission (2 Kings 3:11). When Elisha came to them, he called for a *minstrel*—other translations render the term as *harpist* or *musician*. Only after the musician played did the word of the Lord come to Elisha (3:16). The vital presence of music in the lives of God's people shines through in this passage. While we cannot read Elisha's experience as a prescription for all of God's people, we can observe the significant role that music plays in bringing people into contact with the Creator. As we live and worship today, we would do well to make music a regular part of our spiritual lives, allowing God to use it to draw our hearts closer to Him.

2 Kings 4

Then she called to her husband and said, "Please send me one of the servants and one of the donkeys, that I may run to the man of God and return." —2 Kings 4:22

In the village of Shunem, there lived a woman who regularly fed the prophet Elisha, provided him a place to stay, and birthed a son as a result of the prophet's prayer. When that son died, the woman fell before Elisha in pain and supplication, trusting that he would raise her son from the dead—which he did. This is the kind of trust we all need and desire, isn't it? The kind of conviction that is so practiced, it perseveres whether or not life goes our way. It's a faith that bursts forth with fresh vibrancy as we care for the needs of others. It deals with the trials of life that are sure to come. This faith we all desire and should be striving for is the same devotion the apostle James called us to, a mature faith that evidences itself in our actions, no matter the circumstances of our lives (James 2:23).

2 Kings 5

The he said to him, "Did not my heart go with you, when the man turned from his chariot to meet you? Is it a time to receive money and to receive clothes and olive groves and vineyards and sheep and oxen and male and female servants?" —2 Kings 5:26

Elisha received a visit from a great warrior of Aram, Naaman, who was a leper. Naaman had heard about Elisha's miracle-working and went to Israel in the hope that the prophet would heal him. After being healed, Naaman wanted to thank Elisha with a gift, but the prophet would not accept it (2 Kings 5:16). As Naaman made for home, Elisha's servant Gehazi, who felt that Elisha should have taken *something*, tracked down Naaman and lied in order to get a gift from the healed warrior. Naaman gladly obliged, but when Gehazi returned, Elisha already knew what had happened, his prophetic instinct having taken over. Gehazi hoped that he would benefit from his secret act, but instead, his lies left him with Naaman's leprosy (5:27). His sin had found him out, just as sin continues to do to us today. Though we may act sinfully only in secret, exposure often follows—and with exposure come consequences.

2 Kings 6

So he answered, "Do not fear, for those who are with us are more than those who are with them." —2 Kings 6:16

How should we respond when troubles come upon us? Israel's neighbor Aram had been sending into Israel marauding bands (2 Kings 6:8, 23). However, Elisha's warnings to the king of Israel allowed God's people to defend themselves effectively against these groups of foreign warriors. Frustrated by the failures, Aram's king sent an army to capture Elisha. When Elisha's servant saw Aram's army surrounding the city, he ran to Elisha in terror (6:15). The prophet responded boldly and calmly: "Do not fear" (6:16). It's an oft-repeated biblical exhortation. Why? We have a choice in how we react to troubles that beset us. God calls us to courage. The absence of fear most often indicates the presence of trust. Will we trust God for deliverance and help as Elisha did? Or will we allow fear to dictate our responses to the circumstances around us?

2 Kings 7

Now the king appointed the royal officer on whose hand he leaned to have charge of the gate; but the people trampled on him at the gate, and he died just as the man of God had said, who spoke when the king came down to him. —2 Kings 7:17

In a city beset with food shortages and high prices, Elisha prophesied that all the misfortune would reverse in a single day (2 Kings 7:1). When one of the king's advisors doubted Elisha, the prophet assured him that though the advisor would see the results, he would not share in them (7:2). When the well-supplied Aramean army fled in the night, leaving their ample stores behind, the means were at hand to turn the city's problems around (7:16). In their desperate rush to grab supplies, the people of the city trampled and killed the king's advisor at his post at the city's gate. Elisha's prophecy had come to fruition. The unbelief of the king's advisor led to tragic consequences. When we persist in unbelief, we expose ourselves, not necessarily to literal death but to a loss of blessing and provision that God offers His people.

2 Kings 8

Now Elisha spoke to the woman whose son he had restored to life, saying, "Arise and go with your household, and sojourn wherever you can sojourn; for the LORD has called for a famine, and it will even come on the land for seven years." —2 Kings 8:1

A seven-year famine would descend on the land, Elisha told the Shunammite woman. She would need to take her family away

from God's Promised Land and find a home elsewhere to avoid
the difficulties ahead. God's prophet was advising this woman
to remove herself temporarily from God's promise for the sake
of her family. Her sojourn in the land of the enemy Philistines
promised her life (2 Kings 8:3). The Promised Land, due to
judgment, could make no such provision. As He did with the
Shunammite woman, God has called His people today to sojourn
in the world as we await the return of Christ. As strangers in
the world—though not strangers to God (Ephesians 2:19)—we
have been called to abstain from fleshly desires (1 Peter 2:11).
The Lord, therefore, has called us to purity during this time of
sojourn, even as a spiritual famine rages all around us.

2 Kings 9

*When Jehu came to Jezreel, Jezebel heard of it, and she painted her
eyes and adorned her head and looked out the window. As Jehu
entered the gate, she said, "Is it well, Zimri, your master's murderer?"*
—2 Kings 9:30–31

Ahab and Jezebel led Israel into idolatry and murder like no
other king and queen before them. And though King Ahab humbled himself at the end of his life (1 Kings 21:27), God deemed
that his line needed replacing. So after Ahab died, God called
Jehu to assassinate Ahab's son—the newly installed king—and
his entire family, including Jezebel, Ahab's widow. Always a self-
assured woman, Jezebel held on to her pride to the end. She
painted her face when Jehu came to execute her, that she might
die looking like a queen. She also called Jehu "Zimri," a refer-
ence to another royal assassin in Israel's history whose reign was

short-lived (1 Kings 16:9–10, 15). Jezebel lived in pride, and she died in it. One of the dangers of pride involves the inability to see beyond one's own desires. The prideful person cannot understand his or her evil deeds. Jezebel stands as a beacon reminding us to humble ourselves before it's too late.

2 Kings 10

He said, "Come with me and see my zeal for the LORD." So he made him ride in his chariot. When he came to Samaria, he killed all who remained to Ahab in Samaria, until he had destroyed him, according to the word of the LORD which He spoke to Elijah.

—2 Kings 10:16–17

Jehu was zealous for God. He expressed his zeal by killing off the previous generation of rulers in Israel. Those rulers, Ahab and Jezebel, were among the most wicked in Israel's history. And Jehu acted in response to direct revelation from a prophet of God. Zeal for the Lord in difficult circumstances led Jehu to dramatic actions in stamping out evil. As followers of Jesus, we don't dole out suffering in God's name. Jesus's method for stamping out evil involved taking punishment on Himself, rather than punishing others. As we seek to be passionate about God and the things of God, we would do well to remember that He has not called us to kill our enemies but to turn the other cheek (Matthew 5:39). Our zeal should lead us to engage in dramatic actions, but those actions should always be consistent with the command of Jesus to love our neighbor as ourselves.

2 Kings 11

*Then Jehoiada made a covenant between the LORD and the king and
the people, that they would be the LORD's people, also between the
king and the people.* —2 Kings 11:17

Upon the death of her son the king, the queen mother, Athaliah,
in an effort to take power for herself, had all of her grandchildren killed, save one who secretly escaped (2 Kings 11:1–2). In
the aftermath, only a few knew the location of the young boy,
Joash. Among them was a priest named Jehoiada, and when
Joash turned seven, Jehoiada decided it was time to unveil the
boy as king. With an army of protectors for the boy, Jehoiada had
the queen seized and executed, while Joash was installed as king
over Judah. Jehoiada's first act upon the wicked queen's death
was to consecrate the reign of young Joash, making a covenant
between God and the king and the people (11:17). Strong moral
figures aid the community. Though we may be surrounded by
wickedness, a solid and humble commitment to the ways of God
will benefit us as well as those around us.

2 Kings 12

*Moreover, they did not require an accounting from the men into
whose hand they gave the money to pay to those who did the work,
for they dealt faithfully.* —2 Kings 12:15

As young Joash grew up, he remained true to the principles and
direction of God. When the priests failed to follow Joash's direction to repair the temple, the king called the priests together and
set them to work. The priests collected money and paid workers (2 Kings 12:11–12), but no accounting was asked from the

workers. There existed at this time a culture of mutual trust, in which the people dealt honestly with one another. This attitude in the people came from a leader who trusted his people. Though the people did not always do everything the king told them — they failed to repair the temple in the first place — his trust in them made their laudable dealing with the workers possible. The benefits of trusting others extend far beyond our own well-being. Our trust empowers others to return that trust with faithful work while strengthening our churches and communities in the process.

2 Kings 13

Elisha said to him, "Take a bow and arrows." So he took a bow and arrows. . . . He said, "Open the window toward the east," and he opened it. Then Elisha said, "Shoot!" And he shot. And he said, "The LORD's arrow of victory, even the arrow of victory over Aram; for you will defeat the Arameans at Aphek until you have destroyed them."
—2 Kings 13:15, 17

Elisha had one of the most dramatic ministries of all the Old Testament prophets, matched in his miracle-working only by his predecessor Elijah and, of course, Moses. As Elisha neared death, King Joash of Judah came to visit and mourn the prophet. Always attentive to the needs of God's people, Elisha delivered a word of comfort to the king. Even though he faced death, Elisha's focus pointed outward. How difficult it is for us to follow Elisha's example, even though we might not be facing death ourselves.

Without the distraction of imminent death, turning our attention to the needs and comfort of others should be, technically, easier for us. But self-absorption has a way of pulling us back in. As a result, we must make every effort to fight against that pull, to listen attentively to those around us, and to act swiftly when a need in someone else presents itself.

2 Kings 14

For the LORD saw the affliction of Israel, which was very bitter; for there was neither bond nor free, nor was there any helper for Israel. The LORD did not say that He would blot out the name of Israel from under heaven, but He saved them by the hand of Jeroboam the son of Joash. —2 Kings 14:26–27

Jeroboam II continued the wicked ways of his predecessors when he took over the throne of Israel (2 Kings 14:24). And yet, despite his wickedness, Jeroboam stands as one of the most "successful" kings in Israel's history—extending the borders of his country and in the process pushing back enemies (14:25). But why would God bless a people—from the king on down to the peasants—who had so obviously turned their backs on Him? *Grace*. God decided to extend grace to Israel, illustrating once again that God's grace does not depend on our good deeds but upon God's goodness and kindness toward humanity. The evidences of God's grace are everywhere in the world: the birth of a baby, the presence of food on the table, and success in employment, to name a few. God extends His grace to His creation despite our wickedness. We only need to look for that grace to find it.

2 Kings 15

Pul, king of Assyria, came against the land, and Menahem gave Pul a thousand talents of silver so that his hand might be with him to strengthen the kingdom under his rule. —2 Kings 15:19

Money only goes so far. It can purchase temporary comforts and endless piles of goods, but it cannot bring true and lasting security. Israel learned this lesson during the reign of Menahem. The powerful king of Assyria pushed his army to Israel's doorstep and demanded tribute. The king immediately bowed, hoping that Assyria would help strengthen the kingdom of God's people. The account mentions no moment of consideration by Menahem, no prayer of help offered to the true God. Instead, we only see a willingness to place a greater burden on Menahem's own people in the fleeting hope of buying security (2 Kings 15:20). Purchased security is only temporary, though. When the cash stops flowing, the protection takes flight. Menahem illustrates for us that true and lasting security cannot come through our own devices. Instead, we must rely on God, our only reliable source of true and lasting help.

2 Kings 16

So Ahaz sent messengers to Tiglath-pileser king of Assyria, saying, "I am your servant and your son; come up and deliver me from the hand of the king of Aram and from the hand of the king of Israel, who are rising up against me." —2 Kings 16:7

Ahaz, king of Judah, had forgotten his identity—not in a literal sense, of course. But the king forgot who God had made him to be. When Ahaz faced two armies outside the walls of his capital city, the king did not fall on his knees before the Lord. Neither did the king rush to the temple and demand a sacrifice be made on behalf of his own and the people's sin. Instead, Ahaz sent a message to the king of Assyria, referring to himself as Tiglath-pileser's servant *and* son. Were Ahaz to follow in the footsteps of Judah's ideal king, David, he would have thought of himself as God's son (Psalm 2:7). Instead, Ahaz prostrated himself before a wicked and foreign king and even robbed the temple of God to pay this king (2 Kings 16:8). When we forget our identities and live as people devoted to gods other than Jesus Christ, we leave ourselves open to harsh consequences.

2 Kings 17

So the LORD was very angry with Israel and removed them from His sight; none was left except the tribe of Judah. —2 Kings 17:18

The Lord's anger burned against the northern kingdom of Israel for more than two hundred years—virtually its entire existence. Recording the captivity of Israel, 2 Kings details a lengthy list of sins that led God to evict His people from the land of promise (2 Kings 17:7–17). Vanity, unfaithfulness, and murder dot the landscape of Israel's sin. And yet, the finality of removing the people from the land came only after more than two hundred years of these behaviors. God was nothing if not patient with His people. This passage reminds us that anger is an appropriate response to sin. However, just as God did, that anger must be handled in accordance with justice. We tend to abuse anger—either by bringing it out when it's not called for or by indulging it too much when it is called for. We must remember to direct our anger at actual sin and to model God's patience in bringing out the consequences.

2 Kings 18

For he clung to the LORD; he did not depart from following Him, but kept His commandments, which the LORD had commanded Moses.

—*2 Kings 18:6*

Hezekiah stands as the high point among the last kings of Judah (2 Kings 18:5). When he found himself and his people backed into a corner by the invading Assyrian army, Hezekiah called upon God for help (19:16, 19). Hezekiah's practice models substantive trust in the ability of God to deliver. As such, the writer of 2 Kings states that Hezekiah "clung to the LORD" (18:6). The king's actions reveal that clinging to the Lord is more than a feeling—it involves real action on our part, specifically obedience to God's commands. We have a tendency to refer to our faith in overly emotional terms and imagine that our closeness with God is evidenced in our feelings. However, feelings come and go. When God grants us the gift of faith, it remains. Maybe if we did less talking about our faith and spent more time praying and helping others, God's gift of faith would shine out all the more.

2 Kings 19

"Thus you shall say to Hezekiah king of Judah, 'Do not let your God in whom you trust deceive you saying, "Jerusalem will not be given into the hand of the king of Assyria."'"   —*2 Kings 19:10*

Hezekiah faced a remarkable trial during his reign. The most fearsome army in the entire world seized Judah's greatest cities and threatened even Jerusalem. These Assyrians sought to intimidate Hezekiah and the rest of Judah into giving up their land and following the Assyrians. The Assyrians placed themselves above Israel's God, believing that because they had taken other kingdoms, they would do the same to Judah. These unbelievers sought to plant seeds of doubt in the hearts of Judah's people. Unbelievers will often make claims about the world that sit in direct contrast with what we believers know to be true. And as a result, many believers falter in their trust of God. When confronted with such situations, we must realize that when we have competing claims before us, we have to decide whom to trust. In every case, God—infinite, all-knowing, and present—will be more trustworthy than any person and his or her competing claim.

2 Kings 20

Then Hezekiah said to Isaiah, "The word of the Lord which you have spoken is good." For he thought, "Is it not so, if there will be peace and truth in my days?"   —2 Kings 20:19

Hezekiah was one of Judah's best kings, but he wasn't perfect. After God's victory over the Assyrians, Hezekiah illustrated his shortsightedness. The king arrogantly displayed Judah's treasures to representatives of a nation unknown to Hezekiah—Babylon. Isaiah made Hezekiah aware that his action would yield judgment from those same Babylonians in some future day after Hezekiah's death (2 Kings 20:17–18). The king missed the tragedy in the prophet's pronouncement, choosing to focus only on the promised safety during his own lifetime. Hezekiah's failure to consider the next generation mirrors much of what we see in society today. The prevalence of fractured homes, broken schools, and watered-down churches are all evidence of people's failure to do right by those growing up today. We are responsible to set positive examples for those behind us. When we don't take this responsibility seriously, we leave the next generation a world in which it is even more challenging to live well.

2 Kings 21

But they did not listen, and Manasseh seduced them to do evil more than the nations whom the LORD destroyed before the sons of Israel.
— 2 Kings 21:9

Manasseh's wickedness influenced his people in dramatic ways. After the reign of Hezekiah, Judah stood at a high point of strong leadership. But when Manasseh took over, he followed after all manner of evil that his father never indulged, up to and including defacing the temple, seeing mediums and spiritists, and sacrificing his son in a fire dedicated to a false god (2 Kings 21:6–7). To describe how Manasseh caused the nation to fall, the Bible uses the term *seduced*. Bad leaders seduce their people like certain greedy men seduce naive women for personal gain. Leaders have the potential for significant influence because of their propensity to have followers. As such, we need to expect our leaders to abide by a higher standard of behavior — one that prioritizes the needs of others and remains committed to purity and truth. In this way, God's people will grow stronger and make an even more significant impact.

2 Kings 22

When the king heard the words of the book of the law, he tore his
clothes. —2 Kings 22:11

How often do God's words fall on deaf ears? How often do they
fail to lead us to make real and lasting change in our lives? The
experience of Josiah stands in stark contrast to those who fail
to respond to God's Word. After calling the priests to repair the
temple of the Lord, Josiah received from the high priest a copy of
the books of the Law (Genesis–Deuteronomy) discovered during the cleanup. Immediately, Josiah called for a reading. Upon
hearing the Word of God, the king "tore his clothes," a typical
sign of mourning in the ancient world. The king realized that the
words of God had been lost to him and to his people for many
years, leaving them without a guide to enter into the true worship of God. Josiah shows us that God's words are vital to our
lives spiritually and practically.

2 Kings 23

He did evil in the sight of the LORD, according to all that his fathers
had done. —2 Kings 23:37

Following our parents and grandparents is the easiest sinful path
available to us. We spend immense amounts of time with our
immediate family during our most formative years. As a result,
the potential for adopting some version of their sins is high for
all of us. Avoiding our parents' sins becomes the exception rather
than the rule. The same was true of the kings of Israel and Judah.

More often than not, if a father sold himself out to a life of sin, his son would follow him in those same sins. Jehoiakim was one of the final kings of Judah, and he fit the pattern by following the footsteps of his grandfather, Manasseh. We often struggle to break such patterns of sin, and rightly so. We need to remember that the struggle itself is a good thing, a sign that we have not succumbed completely to generational sin.

2 Kings 24

Surely at the command of the LORD it came upon Judah, to remove them from His sight because of the sins of Manasseh, according to all that he had done. —*2 Kings 24:3*

God had brought judgment upon Judah; they could not blame Babylon or any other foreign power for their misfortune. As a separate kingdom, Judah had nearly five hundred years of opportunity to turn away from their sinful ways. Over and over again, God granted them the grace of faithful rulers who led the people away from idolatry or who repented at the hearing of God's Word. Still, the people persisted in sin. Still, the people embraced gods other than the One who brought them into the land. Still, the people turned from the faithful ways of their father, David. Today, God continues to provide time for repentance. God's people continue to proclaim His Son, Jesus, as the means of forgiveness for our sin. We must ask ourselves and those around us whether we desire to follow the Lord or whether we prefer to take our chances with a coming judgment.

2 Kings 25

They slaughtered the sons of Zedekiah before his eyes, then put out the eyes of Zedekiah and bound him with bronze fetters and brought him to Babylon. —2 Kings 25:7

What a fitting end to a book recounting the sad, pre-exilic history of God's people. Upon Zedekiah's capture, the former king of Israel watched the Babylonians execute his sons. Then the king's own eyes were put out . . . a blind king for a blind people. As a people, they had failed to see the true God and His true way, time and time again. For generations, they chose to follow other gods and pursue their own desires. God was patient with the people, but in an effort to save them from themselves, He brought judgment upon them. God often does the same for us, albeit in lesser ways than portrayed here. But His concern for us is the same as His concern for His Old Testament people: God wants us to follow Him and to become all that He has created us to be. Blind Zedekiah stands and asks: *Do you see?*

First Chronicles

1 Chronicles 1

Adam, Seth, Enosh, . . . — *1 Chronicles 1:1*

In composing a genealogy for the chastened Israelites returning from Babylonian exile, the chronicler traced the people's roots back to the beginning — not just to the beginning of Israel, but to the beginning of all humanity. Haggard and homeless after traveling nearly a thousand miles from Babylon to Judea, the people needed to reestablish their identity as people of the Promised Land. This first involved remembering that they had descended from Adam, that they were, in fact, creatures made in the image of the Creator. This starting point, if embraced, would allow Israel to reestablish itself in the land under the authority of God. Understanding ourselves as creatures made in the image of God has a profound impact on our understanding of our identity. This results in real change in the way we live among others — less selfishness and more kindness, less judgment and more compassion, less hatred and more love.

1 Chronicles 2

These are the sons of Israel: Reuben, Simeon, Levi, Judah, Issachar, Zebulun, Dan, Joseph, Benjamin, Naphtali, Gad and Asher.
— *1 Chronicles 2:1–2*

Displaced from their historic roots in the Promised Land for seventy years, the people of Israel were in danger of forgetting their past. The genealogy in 1 Chronicles 2 links the post-exilic Israelites to the twelve sons of Jacob, who served as the fountainheads of Israel's twelve tribes. Many years prior, after escaping slavery in Egypt, the twelve tribes of Israel prepared to enter and subdue the Promised Land under Joshua. Moses assured them that they had been set apart by God, chosen "for His own possession" from among all people on earth (Deuteronomy 7:6). This chosen people had, therefore, a special mission on earth—to serve as witnesses to God's redemptive power in the world. The apostle Peter made clear that we Christians, in the tradition of Israel, are also a chosen people. This identity compels us to bear witness, by our good deeds, to God's redemptive power in the Messiah, Jesus Christ (1 Peter 2:10–12).

1 Chronicles 3

Now these were the sons of David who were born to him in Hebron: the firstborn was Amnon, by Ahinoam the Jezreelitess; the second was Daniel, by Abigail the Carmelitess. —*1 Chronicles 3.1*

The chronicler highlighted King David in his extensive genealogy, giving David's heritage and lineage far greater treatment than anyone else outside the original heads of the twelve tribes of Israel. David was an important figure for the newly settled Israelites. He, like them, started from a lowly position (1 Samuel 16:10–13). Soon David became great, not just in the eyes of the people but in the eyes of God as well. When, early in his reign, the king expressed a desire to build a temple to the Lord, God promised that David's kingdom would endure forever (2 Samuel 7:16). For a people returning to their land after exile, the mention of David would have reminded them of that promise, restoring confidence in God's plan for His people to endure. We know today that God continues to make eternal provision for believers, a truth that should give us confidence and rest in His perfect plan.

1 Chronicles 4

Now Jabez called on the God of Israel, saying, "Oh that You would bless me indeed and enlarge my border, and that Your hand might be with me, and that You would keep me from harm that it may not pain me!" And God granted him what he requested.

—1 Chronicles 4:10

Not all of the twelve tribes of Israel received equal blessing from God. Of the twelve, Judah received the single-most significant blessing—being the tribe through which the Messiah would come into the world (Genesis 49:10). The story of an otherwise unknown man named Jabez appears amidst a section of Scripture detailing the descendants of Judah. The specific example of Jabez illustrates the blessings of the tribe as a whole, which survived in the land longer than the other tribes. Jabez was the beneficiary of concrete, material blessing from God, who promised the people of Israel in the Mosaic Law that they would be blessed for their faithfulness to Him. We are no longer under the Law, and God has made no such promise to Christians. We can, however, give thanks when God showers His blessings upon us, recognizing the movement of grace that echoes His blessing of Jabez thousands of years ago.

1 Chronicles 5

But they acted treacherously against the God of their fathers and played the harlot after the gods of the peoples of the land, whom God had destroyed before them.   *—1 Chronicles 5:25*

Tragic histories develop when people entertain sin. The descendants of Reuben received from their father the rotten reward of his sinful lifestyle. Though Reuben was the firstborn of Jacob's children, he had relations with one of his father's concubines and forfeited his birthright (1 Chronicles 5:1). Reuben's prominence among the other tribes remained but at no great consequence. Though the tribe had moments of true faith in God, its people turned against Him to worship idols. The people of the tribe of Reuben experienced a downward spiral into sin that ended in their exile (5:19–26). We all know the Reubens of our day, those who seemingly have every advantage, yet fritter it all away with years of indulgence in immoral behavior. Will we follow after Reuben to finish poorly, or will we take the narrower path and get stronger as we go?

1 Chronicles 6

Now these are those whom David appointed over the service of song in the house of the LORD, after the ark rested there.

— 1 Chronicles 6:31

Worship has always been at the center of life for God's faithful people. And God has always made provision for His people to worship. For the bulk of Israel's history, that provision involved the tribe of Levi serving in positions essential to worship—such as ministering at the temple or leading in song. First Chronicles 6 not only traces the genealogy of these Levites but also shows that God divided them according to their tasks and provided places for them to live (1 Chronicles 6:32, 49, 54). Part of God providing a means for His people to worship includes providing individuals to lead the people in worship. Such vital ministry has taken place through the church now for two thousand years, as pastors have led the people in the teaching of Scripture, the singing of songs, and the partaking of the Lord's Supper. As we worship, we thank God for His provision of those leaders.

1 Chronicles 7

Then he went in to his wife, and she conceived and bore a son, and he named him Beriah, because misfortune had come upon his house.
                                                    — 1 Chronicles 7:23

All people suffer, and the Israelites were no exception. First Chronicles 7 recounts the stories of several minor Israelite tribes and, in the process, offers one man as an example of the suffering that characterized the people during their time in the land. Ephraim's children were killed at the hands of Philistine invaders, an event that brings the experience of Job to mind (1 Chronicles 7:21–22). But after mourning, Ephraim and his wife had more children who went on to settle widely and accomplish great feats. Ephraim's descendants persevered despite persecution. The Ephraimites became one of the most numerous of the twelve tribes, and eventually some of their descendants returned to the land after the exile (9:3). Suffering will indeed visit all of us. Ephraim shows us that it doesn't last forever. God always brings deliverance of one kind or another to His people.

1 Chronicles 8

Ner became the father of Kish, and Kish became the father of Saul, and Saul became the father of Jonathan, Malchi-shua, Abinadab, and Eshbaal.   *— 1 Chronicles 8:33*

The extensive genealogy of Benjamin in this chapter serves to highlight Israel's first king, Saul, in the record of God's people as the chronicler builds toward the story of Saul's death at the hands of the Philistines (1 Chronicles 10:1–10). The story of Saul's life and death served as an important cautionary tale for the people, providing a counterpoint in history to the successes of David. More than that, Saul was a reminder to the people after the exile of the kinds of problems that led to their being exiled in the first place. Judah's history under the kings was mixed at best, and the unfaithfulness of leaders and common people led to judgment from God. The dark periods in our own personal histories can serve similar purposes, reminding us of the harsh consequences that come with our sin and motivating us to rely ever more on the grace of God that comes through His Son, Jesus Christ.

1 Chronicles 9

So all Israel was enrolled by genealogies; and behold, they are writ-ten in the Book of the Kings of Israel. And Judah was carried away into exile to Babylon for their unfaithfulness. —1 Chronicles 9:1

First Chronicles 9 brings the genealogy up to the time of the book's writing, recording the names of those who resettled Jerusalem after the exile (1 Chronicles 9:3). In this, the last of nine chapters of genealogy, the chronicler connects the ancients with the contemporary people. Here we see the true value of genealogies—they link us to the past. Just as the Jews were in the land after the exile as a result of their ancestors who originally followed God and settled the land, so too are we Christians fol-lowing Christ today because those before us have been faithful to pass on the message of the gospel, generation after genera-tion. Understanding that invaluable link to history expands our understanding of the church by prompting us to acknowledge those faithful believers who have gone before us. And it increases our confidence in the good news as we see how the Spirit pre-served that message for two thousand years.

1 Chronicles 10

When all Jabesh-gilead heard all that the Philistines had done to Saul, all the valiant men arose and took away the body of Saul and the bodies of his sons and brought them to Jabesh, and they buried their bones under the oak in Jabesh, and fasted seven days.
— 1 Chronicles 10:11–12

First Chronicles opens its narrative section with the tragedy of Saul's death. Though Saul was a weak and disobedient king, Israel rightly mourned the loss of its anointed leader. Saul's body, along with those of three of his sons, lay overnight on Mount Gilboa, exposed to the elements, the animals, and the abusive hands of the enemy. While most of Israel cowered in the wake of Philistine aggression, "valiant men" from the town of Jabesh-gilead retrieved the bodies of Saul and his sons after the Philistines had fastened them to the walls of Beth-shan (1 Samuel 31:8–13). The courage of this small band of men stands in stark contrast to the fear that gripped the rest of God's people. Many Christians, knowingly and unknowingly, operate on the basis of fear. May the bravery of these Israelites inspire Christians today to live with the grit and resolve we need to walk in faith despite our enemy.

1 Chronicles 11

Now these are the heads of the mighty men whom David had, who gave him strong support in his kingdom, together with all Israel, to make him king, according to the word of the LORD concerning Israel.
— 1 Chronicles 11:10

David understood the power of supportive people even from before his days as king over Israel. As Saul pursued David from isolated caves to foreign cities, a group of outsiders and outcasts formed around David, the anointed king (1 Samuel 22:2). Later, as king, David's inner circle included thirty mighty men, a group of his best warriors, men that David could rely on in battle. These men were also instrumental in making David king, according to the chronicler. Part of David's success was directly related to the loyal people God placed around him. God has always used others to place and keep people in the positions He desires for them. For Christians today, God provides support in and through our families, our friends, and the church. No one can go it alone. We should seek out those God has placed in our paths to assist us in becoming the persons God desires us to be.

1 Chronicles 12

Of the sons of Issachar, men who understood the times, with knowledge of what Israel should do, their chiefs were two hundred; and all their kinsmen were at their command. —1 Chronicles 12:32

Knowing the culture in which we live will help us live well in the world. The sons of Issachar understood their culture and, therefore, possessed knowledge that benefitted many. The chronicler lists this group alongside others in Israel who helped David solidify his hold on the kingdom. In other words, the knowledge of the sons of Issachar resulted not in intellectual grandstanding but in decisive action that produced significant results. In the same way, when Christians understand the culture of today, we can benefit our families, our churches, and the communities in which we live. Jesus has called His people to live in the world, though not to be of it (John 17:14–15). We should not then retreat from our culture into isolated "fortresses" or "holy huddles"; rather, we should engage our world as we live out our collective calling to be a holy people (1 Peter 2:9).

1 Chronicles 13

David was afraid of God that day, saying, "How can I bring the ark of God home to me?" — 1 Chronicles 13:12

The hillsides and roadways along the ark's journey to Jerusalem teemed with people who played music, sang songs, and danced in celebration. David had the ark set on a cart and pulled by oxen. This means of transporting the ark was prohibited by God (Exodus 25:13–14). David attempted to accomplish a good deed but in an ungodly fashion . . . and it yielded disastrous consequences. As the cart listed to one side, a man nearby named Uzza, believing the ark was falling to the ground, reached out his hand to stabilize the precious artifact. This clear violation of the Old Testament Law (Numbers 4:15) led to Uzza's immediate death. A pall fell over the celebratory crowd. God's anger had burned against Uzza. Now, David's anger burned against God. Another man had suffered for David's foolish fancy. When we go our own way rather than God's, the consequences can be fierce, both for us and other people.

1 Chronicles 14

They abandoned their gods there; so David gave the order and they were burned with fire. — 1 Chronicles 14:12

With Israel's change in leadership, the Philistines saw an opportunity to strike at the newly enthroned King David, hoping to capitalize on the national weaknesses that come before a king can fully consolidate his power. However, David went up and met the Philistines in battle, having received God's blessing. When Israel won the battle, the Philistines fled, abandoning their idols, which David then burned. How often do we act like the Philistines? Do we treat God like a cheap idol, abandoning Him at the first sign of strife and suffering? Our responses in times of trouble indicate our beliefs about God. When we abandon Him amid difficulties and seek to save ourselves by our own power, we reveal that we think of Him as little more than a carved piece of wood or a sculpted piece of metal, rather than the sovereign Creator of wood, metal, and everything else that exists.

1 Chronicles 15

"Because you did not carry it at the first, the LORD our God made an outburst on us, for we did not seek Him according to the ordinance."
—1 Chronicles 15:13

Staggered by the startling judgment of God upon Uzza (1 Chronicles 13:10), David left the ark of the covenant at a private residence for three months (13:14). The intervening time allowed the king to see the error of his ways—he had not transported the ark according to God's Law. First Chronicles 15 records the result of David's repentance. Obedience replaced disobedience. The king chose Levites to carry the ark according to God's prescription. David's deeds in the aftermath of Uzza's death reveal an important truth: when we falter, we repent of our deeds, not just by a change of mind but also by a change of behavior. David's response shows us that true repentance requires a changed life, a turning in both mind and body from our inclination toward wicked deeds. No doubt David's identity as a man after God's own heart resulted, in part, from his willingness to truly repent.

1 Chronicles 16

He distributed to everyone of Israel, both man and woman, to everyone a loaf of bread and a portion of meat and a raisin cake.
—1 Chronicles 16:3

An appetizing aroma emanated from the area in front of the tent where David instructed the Levites to place the ark. The people made offerings to the Lord in honor of the ark's delivery into Israel's capital, Jerusalem. Afterward, David extended a blessing to the people who had gathered for the ceremony (1 Chronicles 16:2). However, David was not satisfied with a merely spiritual benefit for the people. He followed his verbal blessing with something more tangible—he gave everyone bread, meat, and raisin cakes. David understood the power of material blessings. He understood that food filling a hungry stomach communicates appreciation and care in a way that words can never match. David's act foreshadows the New Testament teaching of James, who exhorted believers to honor the deep connection between faith and deeds (James 2:15–16). What material blessings accompany the spiritual blessings we offer people?

1 Chronicles 17

"And now it has pleased You to bless the house of Your servant, that it may continue forever before You; for You, O LORD, have blessed, and it is blessed forever."　　　　　*—1 Chronicles 17:27*

David faltered during his time as king, sometimes in profoundly damaging ways. In response to each of those failures, he oriented his life toward God. When David sinned, he repented (Psalm 51:1–4). And when life went well, he looked for opportunities to show his gratefulness to God. After David expressed his desire to build a temple to house the ark of the covenant (1 Chronicles 17:1–2), God made a covenant with David that promised the blessing and eternal existence of David's line ruling over God's people—a promise ultimately fulfilled in David's descendant, Jesus Christ. God's eternal blessing of David's line despite their failures mirrors His blessing of eternal salvation upon believers today despite our failures. Though we fail, God will bless us with salvation when we repent and believe, when we link our lives with Christ through faith in His redeeming work (Mark 1:15).

1 Chronicles 18

So David reigned over all Israel; and he administered justice and righteousness for all his people.   —1 Chronicles 18:14

Often when our thoughts turn to justice, they revolve around ensuring that we personally receive just treatment. David operated on a different scale. As king, he could have chosen a path in which his desires for justice in his own life trumped all other concerns. The chronicler shows that once he established his kingdom, David instead turned his attention outward. The new king sought out justice for his people, treating them in accordance with righteousness. David operated in the way God operates. All of God's people should mimic David in his pursuit to make the world as it should be, rather than being content with its fallen state. Administering justice and righteousness means acting in tangible ways to bring life to others—feeding a hungry child, encouraging peace amidst conflict, and exhibiting purity in an impure world. Will we follow in David's footsteps, or will we sit back and passively allow injustice and unrighteousness to dominate our world?

1 Chronicles 19

Now when Joab saw that the battle was set against him in front and in the rear, he selected from all the choice men of Israel and they arrayed themselves against the Arameans. . . . He said, "If the Arameans are too strong for me, then you shall help me; but if the sons of Ammon are too strong for you, then I will help you."

—1 Chronicles 19:10, 12

Looking to foster a friendly connection with his neighbors, David sent goodwill messengers to the Ammonites after their king died (1 Chronicles 19:2). However, Ammonite suspicions about the motives of Israel's conquering king led them to insult the messengers and seek a fight against David. To strengthen their numbers, the Ammonites hired mercenaries, the Arameans, and the two groups of soldiers surrounded the Israelite army outside the town of Medeba (19:7). Israel's military commander, Joab, then divided his army—one group facing the Arameans, one facing the Ammonites. Joab's direction to help one another gave his army a guiding principle as they entered battle: two are better than one (Ecclesiastes 4:9–10). Indeed, we are always stronger when we come to each other's aid, a truth that applies far beyond the battlefield. Look for opportunities to stand against the rampant individualism of our world. Instead, stand with others against forces of injustice, deceit, and wickedness.

1 Chronicles 20

These were descended from the giants in Gath, and they fell by the hand of David and by the hand of his servants. *—1 Chronicles 20:8*

When David took over as king of Israel, the instability of life on the country's borders threatened the security of God's people.

Therefore, David fought off the Ammonites east of the Jordan and later the Philistines to the southwest. Among the Philistines, David discovered relatives of Goliath, people whose physical stature stood out from both the Israelites and their Philistine counterparts. These physically imposing specimens threatened Israel's way of life by inciting fear throughout Israel's communities. And yet, David led his people with courage against these giants, slaying them to provide a measure of peace and tranquility in that portion of his country. Just as David slayed the physical giants in his life, we can face the metaphorical giants that threaten us, including addictions, struggles with anger, and deep depressions. God has not promised us complete and final victory on earth, but He has promised to walk those vales of darkness alongside us (Psalm 23:4).

1 Chronicles 21

Then Satan stood up against Israel and moved David to number Israel.   —*1 Chronicles 21:1*

A story also recorded in 2 Samuel 24:1–25, David's desire to hold a census in Israel takes on a different character in 1 Chronicles 21. Before recounting David's sin, the chronicler mentions that Satan "moved" David to undertake the census. However, when David later realized his sin, he took full responsibility for it (1 Chronicles 21:8, 17). Though David had been influenced by a supernaturally powerful person, he did not seek to pin the blame for his act on Satan. We believe Satan continues his destructive activity in our world. But his activity doesn't somehow absolve us from responsibility for our actions. When we sin, we choose to follow the path of wickedness. When we sin, we act. David's confession, recognizing his own culpability despite Satan's role, can therefore serve as an example to us that we not blame our own sinful actions on forces or people other than ourselves.

1 Chronicles 22

So David gave orders to gather the foreigners who were in the land of Israel, and he set stonecutters to hew out stones to build the house of God. David prepared large quantities of iron to make the nails for the doors of the gates and for the clamps, and more bronze than could be weighed; and timbers of cedar logs beyond number, for the Sidonians and Tyrians brought large quantities of cedar timber to David.

—1 Chronicles 22:2–4

God's people have always had a tendency to retreat from the rest of the world. We often close off ourselves in an act of protection from outsiders. However, at the height of Israel's history, God's people approached outsiders much differently. Rather than retreating from their neighbors, they engaged. King David desired to build the temple, but the Lord prevented it, allowing David only the opportunity to gather materials for his son Solomon to begin construction later (2 Chronicles 17:4). How did David gather his materials? He looked beyond the Israelites, contracting with foreigners living in Israel to cut stone and receiving timber from his Sidonian and Tyrian neighbors to the north. As believers living in the world today, we need not isolate ourselves. Instead, we have the opportunity, like David, to interact with those outside our circle of belief. In doing so, we can shine the light of the gospel into the lives of people who desperately need it.

1 Chronicles 23

Now when David reached old age, he made his son Solomon king over Israel. And he gathered together all the leaders of Israel with the priests and the Levites. —1 Chronicles 23:1–2

Near death in his old age, David could not help himself: he looked to the future. He wanted to leave the nation in the best condition possible. David knew that if a nation's worship practices were in order, the nation would be in order. Therefore, the king gathered the leadership of Israel around him and made specific arrangements for the priests and Levites, those chosen by God to lead Israel in worship. David shifted their responsibilities from carrying and setting up the movable tabernacle to caring for the worship space in its permanent place, the temple. David's actions underline for us the centrality of worship in the lives of God's people. Further, David shows us that worship's importance extends not only to ourselves, but to the next generation as well. When it comes to worship, we should look beyond ourselves and make sure that we pass on Christian practices to our children and grandchildren.

1 Chronicles 24

Thus they were divided by lot, the one as the other; for they were officers of the sanctuary and officers of God, both from the descendants of Eleazar and the descendants of Ithamar. —1 Chronicles 24:5

Community has always been a part of God's ordering of society. People make their lives together with others and, in the process, find help bearing their burdens. When David divided the Levites according to their job responsibilities, he implicitly acknowledged the necessity of community. No single Levite would be expected to do every job in leading the people to worship the true God. Instead, each group combined with other groups to accomplish the variety of tasks that proper worship required. David's organizational act of dividing the Levites underlined humanity's need for others in an especially appropriate context. What better place to acknowledge such a need than in worship? In worship, we testify that we cannot go it alone, that we need God to save and strengthen us for the length of our lives. Rather than separate a unified people into competing groups, David's act allowed people to come together and work effectively toward a common goal.

1 Chronicles 25

All these were under the direction of their father to sing in the house of the LORD, with cymbals, harps and lyres, for the service of the house of God. Asaph, Jeduthun and Heman were under the direction of the king. — 1 Chronicles 25:6

David served not only as Israel's king but also as the nation's most prolific psalmist. Through these sacred songs, the king offered prayer to his merciful God for both deliverance and praise. With psalm-writing such a large part of David's life, his concern for the use of music in the worship of God should come as no surprise. When David gathered the Levites together, he assigned one group of them to take responsibility for incorporating music into the worship at the temple that David's son Solomon would construct.

David understood that responding to God involved more than the ability to rattle off propositions about God. A truly human response to God involves the heart, and good music works wonders in awakening the hearts of believers lulled to sleep by the comforts and routines of life. Let us make David's cry our own: "Awake, my soul! Awake, harp and lyre!" (Psalm 57:8 NIV).

1 Chronicles 26

To these divisions of the gatekeepers, the chief men, were given duties like their relatives to minister in the house of the LORD. They cast lots, the small and the great alike, according to their fathers' households, for every gate.   *—1 Chronicles 26:12–13*

With the construction of the temple set to take place during Solomon's reign, King David took it upon himself to appoint workers to specific jobs within the future house of worship. Israel needed people to serve as gatekeepers for the complex, opening the doors in the morning to the public who were coming to worship (1 Chronicles 9:23–27). These gatekeepers would also secure the doors at night, protecting the implements of worship from those with unsavory motives. While the job of the gatekeepers involved the physical temple, the work carried with it a spiritual function as well: these men provided an opportunity for the people of God to worship. They opened the way for the people to humble themselves before God. We all need people like this in our lives, people who mark the way to a healthy relationship with our Creator and Lord.

1 Chronicles 27

Also Jonathan, David's uncle, was a counselor, a man of under-standing, and a scribe; and Jehiel the son of Hachmoni tutored the king's sons. — *1 Chronicles 27:32*

David appointed workers to all manner of positions in his kingdom. But for roles nearest him, the king relied on only the sharpest minds. David knew that he would need the wisest counsel when it came to making the big decisions for the nation of Israel. Having someone like his uncle Jonathan, whom the chronicler describes as "a man of understanding," would have given David confidence in those critical moments of decision. Most of us will never rule as kings, but that does not mean we don't have need of wise counsel. And yet, how many times do we consider only our own counsel when making choices? David was sharp enough to look ahead and take the appropriate steps to ensure he would make godly choices. Each of us must con-sider the people from whom we receive advice. Do they provide refreshment with understanding, or are they more like empty vessels without the capacity to ease our thirst for wisdom?

1 Chronicles 28

"So now, in the sight of all Israel, the assembly of the Lord, and in the hearing of our God, observe and seek after all the commandments of the Lord your God so that you may possess the good land and bequeath it to your sons after you forever." — *1 Chronicles 28:8*

As David prepared to hand over the kingdom to his son Solomon, the aging king gathered his people to him at Jerusalem. From beneath the graying hair that his son would later associate with righteousness (Proverbs 16:31), David charged his people to live in accordance with God's commands so that they would possess the land forever. The results of following after God were tangible. The Israelites would have the privilege of passing on the land to their children. David's promise of a tangible inheritance for God's people reminds us that we too have a tangible hope. We look forward to the time after Jesus returns, when He will reign from Jerusalem and His resurrected followers will live throughout the earth. We need not relegate our hope to some wish for a disembodied existence of floating through the clouds. Instead, we hope to live in a world where everything is as it was created to be.

1 Chronicles 29

Then the people rejoiced because they had offered so willingly,
for they made their offering to the LORD with a whole heart, and
King David also rejoiced greatly. —1 Chronicles 29:9

After David had told the assembly of Israelites of all the materials he had gathered in preparation for building the temple, the people responded to his act of generosity with one of their own. Wholeheartedly, they gave from their own personal provisions. Gold, silver, and jewels poured into the burgeoning temple treasury. We should all take note of David's wisdom here as a leader among the people. Rather than compel the people to give, David first spent his energy gathering a sizable amount of wealth and supplies for the temple's construction (1 Chronicles 29:2). He led the people by example, sacrificing his own time and funds without complaint. The result? The people gave willingly and abundantly, which led all of them, David included, to rejoice in the greatness of their God. Will we lead others in sacrificing without complaint? Will we open the way for rejoicing or close off others with despair?

Second Chronicles

2 Chronicles 1

Then Solomon and all the assembly with him went to the high place which was at Gibeon, for God's tent of meeting was there, which Moses the servant of the LORD had made in the wilderness.

—2 Chronicles 1:3

King Solomon and the assembly worshiped the same God to whom Moses had bowed many years earlier. And the tabernacle that Solomon and the people approached, Moses had made while Israel wandered for years in the wilderness. As God's people moved from place to place, they carried the tabernacle, which signified the Lord's presence with them. Now, as King Solomon looked forward to constructing a permanent house for the Lord, he reminded the Israelites of the Lord's faithfulness to them throughout all generations. Christians today serve the same God as Moses and King Solomon did. And just as He delivered His people from slavery through the divided sea, provided supernatural sustenance, and dwelled with them, the Lord saves believers from bondage to sin, meets our needs, and lives in the hearts of His people, the church. Christians today must continually look back and remember the Lord's consistent record of faithfulness.

2 Chronicles 2

"The house which I am about to build will be great, for greater is our God than all the gods."

—2 Chronicles 2:5

The young King Solomon possessed zeal for the Lord—zeal that would help him build God's temple. Because Solomon believed that the Lord ruled over heaven and earth and that all other "gods" were powerless before Him, Solomon proclaimed God's incomparability wherever and whenever he could. When he wrote to Hiram, king of Tyre, requesting wood and workers to build God's house, Solomon used that letter as an occasion to exalt the Lord. Indeed, only an all-powerful God could keep His promise to King David that his son would build God's temple in Jerusalem. In all situations, God's people must declare His praises! Just as King Solomon shared with King Hiram about God's greatness, Christians should notice and proclaim God's power and mercy with our coworkers, friends, and family. The relationships that God orchestrates in our lives give us divine opportunities to tell others about the grace He offers through Jesus Christ.

2 Chronicles 3

Now he made the room of the holy of holies: its length across the width of the house was twenty cubits, and its width was twenty cubits; and he overlaid it with fine gold, amounting to 600 talents.
—2 Chronicles 3:8

When the Lord told King Solomon to construct the temple, Solomon used the most luxurious materials he could find. Expensive cypress wood, carved with palm trees and cherubim, comprised the main room. Precious stones adorned the entire temple. And everything, from the porch to the beams, the thresholds, the walls, the doors, and the holy of holies— *everything*—was covered with gold, about twenty-three tons of it! Nothing could match the temple's splendor. The exalted Lord of the universe deserves nothing less than the best! And God asks

Christians to adorn our hearts—His home—with the pure gold of love and the precious jewels of grace, obedience, and generosity. As we build our lives according to God's Word and invest our spiritual resources in others, God's people—His church—will begin to look more and more like God's dwelling place each day.

2 Chronicles 4

He also made ten basins in which to wash, and he set five on the right side and five on the left to rinse things for the burnt offering; but the sea was for the priests to wash in. —2 *Chronicles 4:6*

In the Old Testament, ritual washing was an important part of worship. God directed Moses to build a bronze basin and to place it between the tent of meeting and the altar (Exodus 30:18). And He commanded the priests to wash themselves as well as the animals before making sacrifices (Leviticus 1:13; 16:28). According to God's instructions, King Solomon had the temple workers build huge metal basins for that purpose. In the Mosaic Law, God's commands to maintain external cleanliness pointed to His people's need for internal cleansing. God still cares about purity today. Thankfully, Christians don't have to sacrifice ritually pure bulls and goats to cover our sin. Jesus Christ, our great High Priest, shed His own blood to provide permanent cleansing for all who believe in Him (Hebrews 9:11–14). As believers in Christ, let's show the Lord how much we love Him by worshiping Him with purity.

2 Chronicles 5

When the trumpeters and the singers were to make themselves heard with one voice to praise and to glorify the LORD, and when they lifted up their voice accompanied by trumpets and cymbals and instruments of music, and when they praised the LORD saying, "He indeed is good for His lovingkindness is everlasting," then the house, the house of the LORD, was filled with a cloud.   *—2 Chronicles 5:13*

Music lifts our spirits. As beautiful notes fill the air, music fills our hearts with joy. God intended much of Old Testament poetry, especially the psalms, to be sung with an entire orchestra of instruments. As King Solomon and all Israel celebrated the completion of God's temple, they rejoiced with song. God cared so much about melody that He dedicated a group of people — the Levitical singers and musicians — to lead the congregation. They grabbed their trumpets, harps, lyres, and cymbals and belted out God's praise: "He indeed is good for His lovingkindness is everlasting" (2 Chronicles 5:13). When God's people exalt Him with impassioned music and grateful hearts, He is pleased. As Christians attend worship services, we should remember that we stand in a long tradition of musical praise. When we realize God's goodness, we should sing to Him. And when others need encouragement, we should share His melody of praise (Colossians 3:16).

2 Chronicles 6

"But will God indeed dwell with mankind on the earth? Behold, heaven and the highest heaven cannot contain You; how much less this house which I have built." — *2 Chronicles 6:18*

As King Solomon conducted the temple dedication service, he praised God for His faithfulness and asked Him to keep His covenant with King David for generations to come. Solomon prayed for mercy and asked God to listen as His people prayed from His temple. But in the middle of the king's prayer, it must have hit him — *I have just finished building a house for the God of the universe.* King Solomon couldn't fathom how an all-powerful, transcendent God could dwell among the human beings He created. Why would God want to interact with self-centered, fickle people? Philippians 2 gives an answer to King Solomon's question — God is humble. God the Son humbled Himself, added humanity to His deity, and gave Himself for sinful people. Not only does God hear believers' prayers for help, guidance, and comfort, Jesus Christ experienced what it felt like to need His Father. Thank God today for His humility!

2 Chronicles 7

"[If] My people who are called by My name humble themselves and pray and seek My face and turn from their wicked ways, then I will hear from heaven, will forgive their sin and will heal their land."
— *2 Chronicles 7:14*

Just as a new mother attentively listens to the coos and cries of her newborn, the Lord listened attentively as His people called out to Him from the temple. After King Solomon dedicated the Lord's house, God reminded Solomon that His grace always outweighs

His people's sin. Hundreds of years earlier, God gave His people the Mosaic Law in order to set them apart from the surrounding nations. And now that God's temple stood in Jerusalem, the Lord promised that whenever His people transgressed His commands and cried out for mercy from the temple, He would respond. God still extends endless grace to His people. Christians today don't have to confess our sins from a specific location. As believers, we direct our prayers for grace to the Father, through Jesus Christ, who gives generously. So when we sin, let's approach our merciful Father quickly and keep short accounts with Him.

2 Chronicles 8

Then Solomon brought Pharaoh's daughter up from the city of David to the house which he had built for her, for he said, "My wife shall not dwell in the house of David king of Israel, because the places are holy where the ark of the LORD has entered." — 2 Chronicles 8:11

It seems a little coldhearted for a husband to ask his new wife to live in a separate house. But that's exactly what Solomon did after he married Pharaoh's daughter. King Solomon made a political alliance with the king of Egypt and married his daughter to seal the deal. But King Solomon didn't mix politics and religion. He built a separate house for Pharaoh's daughter in order to maintain the sanctity of the palace and the temple. King Solomon didn't want his new bride, a foreigner, to pollute the places where the ark of the covenant, and the Lord's presence, had been. Today, God's presence dwells in believers. Just as King Solomon went to great lengths to keep his palace holy, Christians must remove from their lives anything that does not belong so that the Holy Spirit can work unfettered. Do we, as Christ-followers, place any human relationship above our relationship with Him?

2 Chronicles 9

And Solomon slept with his fathers and was buried in the city of his father David; and his son Rehoboam reigned in his place.
—2 Chronicles 9:31

When Adam and Eve listened to Satan, their sin introduced death into the world. Every time someone dies, we're reminded that things aren't yet how they should be. Death is the great equalizer—the strong and the weak, the king and the peasant pass from this life. The chronicler recorded that King Solomon "slept," or died, and was buried in the City of David. Though Solomon didn't live a perfect life, he trusted in God and depended on His promises. While death remains a tragedy, hope accompanies the passing of God's saints. And for His people, God graciously lessens the blow of sin's consequence. Just as we pass from wakefulness to sleep each night, we have the hope that we will not sleep forever. We will get up in the morning and face a new day. Likewise, when believers die, we know that we will wake again—with imperishable bodies, immune to sickness, pain, and death (1 Corinthians 15:50–57).

2 Chronicles 10

They spoke to him, saying, "If you will be kind to this people and please them and speak good words to them, then they will be your servants forever."
—2 Chronicles 10:7

When Solomon's son Rehoboam became king, he inherited his father's policies of forced labor and high taxes. As King Rehoboam took the throne, his weary citizens saw an opportunity for their burdens to be lifted, and they approached Rehoboam and asked for relief. Unsure how to handle their plea, King Rehoboam asked the elders for advice, and these wise, God-fearing men instructed him to grant the citizens' request. The elders assured the king that his kindness would win the people's allegiance forever. Kindness endears hearts and binds them together. God's kindness—His gracious response to a weary heart—draws people to repentance (Romans 2:4). Just as King Rehoboam's citizens faced physical and financial burdens—and would have responded well to kindness—there are those in our lives who need a kind, rather than a caustic, response from us (Proverbs 25:15).

2 Chronicles 11

Rehoboam lived in Jerusalem and built cities for defense in Judah.
—2 Chronicles 11:5

Not long after he began to rule over Judah, King Rehoboam amassed his troops and planned to march against Jeroboam, king of Israel. After God's prophet rebuked Rehoboam for trying to attack Israel, he relented. And God gave Rehoboam a short period of peace. Rather than sit back and waste the warless time God had given him, King Rehoboam rebuilt and fortified fifteen towns in Judah; stocked them with food, oil, and wine; and hired capable officers to manage supplies and respond to threats. The king of Judah used peacetime to build strong defenses. Likewise, Christians shouldn't use easy times as opportunities to coast spiritually. When God gives us rest, let's use that time to build up our spiritual defenses. Let's spend more time reading God's Word, praying for ourselves and interceding for others, and engaging in spiritual fellowship with Christian friends. Then, when hard times come, we will be ready.

2 Chronicles 12

"But they will become his slaves so that they may learn the difference between My service and the service of the kingdoms of the countries."
—2 Chronicles 12:8

After King Rehoboam fortified the cities of Judah and Benjamin and attained wealth and strength, he got lazy and forgot about God. King Rehoboam relied on his own power, overlooked his need for God, and disobeyed God's commands. And along with the king, all of God's people forsook His Law. Therefore, in order to remind Rehoboam and all Israel of God's gracious Law and loving rule, the Lord allowed cruel King Shishak of Egypt to invade Judah. Shishak's invasion, violence, and plunder contrasted with the Lord's mercy. Human beings have the tendency to forget God when life is easy. But the Lord often uses tragedy, poverty, and heartache to remind us of His kindness and to bring us back to Him. Christians must continually submit to the Lord's kind but sovereign rule. We must remember our desperate need for God's guidance and fight our tendency to rely on our own wisdom.

2 Chronicles 13

Abijah began the battle with an army of valiant warriors, 400,000 chosen men, while Jeroboam drew up in battle formation against him with 800,000 chosen men who were valiant warriors.
—2 Chronicles 13:3

God likes bad odds. King Abijah of Judah and his 400,000 warriors faced King Jeroboam of Israel and his 800,000 troops on the battlefield. Abijah warred with the people of Israel because they had defected from God's true leader. The Lord had promised to rule His people through King David's lineage, but Jeroboam ruled over Israel. Abijah intended to win back Israel and reunite the two nations under the leadership of David's descendants. King Abijah's military had half as many men as Jeroboam's army, but Abijah declared his trust in God to give Judah the victory. God's power on behalf of His people shines brightest when the odds are stacked against them. When Christians face overwhelming challenges, we should trust in the Lord's sovereign ability to come through. When finances are tight and the numbers just won't work, God will provide for our needs—which may include, at times, redefining them. Then, when God beats the odds, He gets the glory!

2 Chronicles 14

Asa and the people who were with him pursued them as far as Gerar; and so many Ethiopians fell that they could not recover, for they were shattered before the LORD and before His army. And they carried away very much plunder. —2 Chronicles 14:13

King Asa and his army of 580,000 soldiers faced an army double its size. Zerah, king of Ethiopia, attacked Judah with his million-man army. Asa recognized his own powerlessness in the face of such strength. But rather than retreat in fear, King Asa called out to the Lord, and God gave Judah victory over the massive Ethiopian army. But as God fought and the Ethiopians fled, King Asa and his troops didn't just stand by and watch the Ethiopians run away—they picked up their weapons and pursued Zerah's troops. When waiting for the Lord to act on our behalf, Christians shouldn't sit back and do nothing. Patience doesn't equal inactivity. For example, if we're waiting for the Lord to meet our financial needs, we should still live modestly and practice stewardship. And while waiting for God's help as we overcome temptation, we should actively search Scripture and seek accountability. Even prayer is an active pursuit.

2 Chronicles 15

Now the Spirit of God came on Azariah the son of Oded.
— 2 Chronicles 15:1

In the Old Testament, the Spirit of God, the third person of the Trinity, "came on" the prophets and empowered them to speak on God's behalf. The prophet Azariah came to King Asa and told Asa that if he pursued the Lord, the Lord would protect him. But if Asa turned his back on God, then God would discipline him. This Spirit-given warning left King Asa without excuse when, later in life, he trusted in the king of Aram instead of the Lord (2 Chronicles 16:7). The Holy Spirit no longer "comes on" people, speaking God's special revelation through them. But God's Spirit inspired the writers of the Old and New Testaments, who gave us God's trustworthy, error-free Word — the Bible. And the Spirit empowers believers to understand and to share His Word with others. Thank God that the Holy Spirit now permanently indwells Christians when we trust in Jesus Christ.

2 Chronicles 16

In the thirty-ninth year of his reign Asa became diseased in his feet. His disease was severe, yet even in his disease he did not seek the Lord, but the physicians.
— 2 Chronicles 16:12

Patterns of behavior are hard to break but not impossible. Once we start eating healthy, it's easier to keep going. But if we consume a candy bar each day, it will likely sabotage our healthy eating habit. For the first thirty-five years of his reign, King Asa was in the habit of prayerfully trusting God. But toward the end of his reign, Asa broke his prayer habit, and his trust in God waned. When Asa faced war with Israel, he begged the king of Aram, not the Lord, to help him. And when King Asa developed a deadly foot disease, he did not seek God but the physicians. God is always faithful. As Christians, we should develop the habit of seeking the Lord and trusting Him in every circumstance. The God of the universe can handle even the most difficult challenges. Believers must develop a routine of prayer, and we must train ourselves to regularly take in God's Word.

2 Chronicles 17

They taught in Judah, having the book of the law of the LORD with them; and they went throughout all the cities of Judah and taught among the people. —2 Chronicles 17:9

Doctrine is essential to the life of God's people. King Jehoshaphat understood that the fear of the Lord springs from the knowledge of His Law. And God had promised to bless His people if they obeyed His Law (Deuteronomy 5:33). Jehoshaphat loved the Lord and His Law, and he wanted God's blessing to rest on the inhabitants of Judah. Jehoshaphat sent a group of political and religious leaders on a mission throughout Judah to teach the Mosaic Law to all the people. Jesus Christ commands believers today to love God with our hearts, souls, minds, and strength (Mark 12:29–30). But in order to obey this command, we must know and love God's Word. As Christ-followers learn biblical truth, we will learn God's desires and begin to think like Him (Romans 12:1–2). And as Scripture transforms us, all believers will be able to encourage each other with God's Word (1 Peter 2:9–10).

153

2 Chronicles 18

But Jehoshaphat said, "Is there not yet a prophet of the LORD here that we may inquire of him?" —2 *Chronicles 18:6*

The best defense against a lie is to know the truth. When King Ahab called in four hundred prophets to tell him whether or not to go to war against Aram, Ahab didn't care that all the prophets spoke lies. But when Jehoshaphat, king of Judah, heard the words of the false prophets, he recognized that they didn't speak for God. He knew the voice of God well enough to spot an imposter. So he asked King Ahab to bring in a true prophet of the Lord to speak God's Word concerning war with Aram. As Christians, we don't have to study every distortion of biblical truth in order to spot heresy. Believers in Christ must learn God's Word and know it well enough to recognize its distortion. The Holy Spirit will help believers develop discernment for direction as we prayerfully study God's Word inside and out.

2 Chronicles 19

"Now then let the fear of the LORD be upon you; be very careful what you do, for the LORD our God will have no part in unrighteousness or partiality or the taking of a bribe." —2 *Chronicles 19:7*

King Jehoshaphat wanted all the people of Judah to obey God's Law, so he instituted reforms. He already had sent teachers of the Mosaic Law to help the people understand God's character. Then Jehoshaphat set up judges in the cities of Judah to apply God's Law to the peoples' disputes. He charged the judges to allow their fear of the Lord to inform their decisions. And if any of the judges showed favoritism or took a bribe, God punished them. God hates partiality and bribes because they "[blind] the eyes of the wise and [pervert] the words of the righteous" (Deuteronomy 16:19). In the New Testament, Jesus rebuked the Pharisees for giving preference to the rich. Christians should follow Christ's example of impartiality. The book of James reminds us that favoritism distorts justice and prevents individuals from giving and receiving grace (James 2:1–13). God doesn't play favorites, so why should we?

2 Chronicles 20

"'You need not fight in this battle; station yourselves, stand and see the salvation of the LORD on your behalf, O Judah and Jerusalem.' Do not fear or be dismayed; tomorrow go out to face them, for the LORD is with you." —2 Chronicles 20:17

Why fight when God has already won the battle? When the Moabites, Ammonites, and Meunites threatened Judah, King Jehoshaphat and all of Judah fasted and asked the Lord to intervene. Jehoshaphat called on God to remember His covenant with Abraham and to protect the people from their enemies. And God responded. The Lord told the king to lead out his troops to face the enemy, but instead of raising their weapons, they were to stand and watch God's salvation. Jesus Christ has already won the battle against sin and death. We can't fight to earn our salvation, nor can we protect ourselves from Satan's attacks without God's help. The apostle Paul encouraged Christians to arm themselves with God's Word and prayer and to trust the indwelling Spirit to protect us from the enemy's blows. Then, once we have put on our armor, all we have to do is stand, trusting in God's salvation.

2 Chronicles 21

He was thirty-two years old when he became king, and he reigned in Jerusalem eight years; and he departed with no one's regret, and they buried him in the city of David, but not in the tombs of the kings.
—2 Chronicles 21:20

Scoundrels aren't missed when they die. Righteous Jehoshaphat's oldest son, Jehoram, took over as king of Judah following his father's death. After Jehoram claimed the throne, he murdered his six brothers in cold blood so they wouldn't threaten his power. King Jehoram then married one of Ahab's daughters, and together they worshiped idols. So God punished Jehoram and gave him a terminal and painful bowel disease. After his death, nobody gave Jehoram the customary burial or the honorary fire fit for the kings. While it may seem easy to dismiss Jehoram as the scoundrel he was, his life and death give us pause. God expects His leaders—and all Christians—to live holy lives. Unrepentance even in the hearts of believers may result in premature death (1 Corinthians 5:5).

2 Chronicles 22

[Ahaziah] also walked in the ways of the house of Ahab, for his mother was his counselor to do wickedly. *—2 Chronicles 22:3*

King Ahaziah didn't have much of a chance. It's hard enough to swim against the tide of cultural pressure. But when your own mother pushes you toward evil, it's nearly impossible not to sink into sin. After Ahaziah succeeded his father, Jehoram, as king of Judah, Ahaziah's mother, Athaliah, counseled him as he carried out his royal duties. An expert in idol worship and self-seeking behavior, Athaliah influenced King Ahaziah to walk in the evil ways of King Ahab. Ahaziah eventually married a daughter in Ahab's family—a woman much like his mother. Unlike Ahaziah's home, the Christian home should provide sanctuary from the wickedness so prevalent in our culture and should create an atmosphere conducive to spiritual growth. Parents should model to their children how to honor the Lord and apply His truth to their lives. Only then will young believers learn how to swim against the strong cultural current of evil.

2 Chronicles 23

She looked, and behold, the king was standing by his pillar at the entrance, and the captains and the trumpeters were beside the king. And all the people of the land rejoiced and blew trumpets, the singers with their musical instruments leading the praise. Then Athaliah tore her clothes and said, "Treason! Treason!" —2 Chronicles 23:13

Athaliah wanted absolute power! After her son Ahaziah died, Athaliah planned to take over his royal duties. She devised a plan to make sure that no other potential successors would arise and strip her of power—she killed them all. With no competition for control, she ruled over Judah for six years. Athaliah forgot that only God has—and can handle—absolute power. Those who claw their way to the top, squashing everyone beneath them, clearly have not bowed to the only Sovereign Lord. As Christians who acknowledge God's providence and power to accomplish His will, we bow to Him first and submit our wills to His. We acknowledge God as sovereign over all things. If the Lord allows us to exercise a measure of power over others, let's wield it with grace, remembering that God will hold us accountable.

2 Chronicles 24

All the officers and all the people rejoiced and brought in their levies and dropped them into the chest until they had finished.

—2 Chronicles 24:10

When tax time rolls around, nobody squeals with joy as they write their checks to the government. But the inhabitants of Judah rejoiced when King Joash commanded them to bring their tax money to the temple in Jerusalem. God's law instructed the people to support the work of the priests and Levites at the tabernacle. Moses gathered money from the Israelites through a census, through the payment of personal vows, and through voluntary offerings (Exodus 30:14; Leviticus 27:1–8). But after several godless kings failed to gather taxes to support the temple, King Joash reenergized God's people to follow God's Law. The New Testament doesn't impose taxes on Christians today, but the Lord still requires His people to give liberally to the work of the church. And joy should motivate our giving as we seek to reflect God's generous character (2 Corinthians 9:7).

2 Chronicles 25

Now after Amaziah came from slaughtering the Edomites, he brought the gods of the sons of Seir, set them up as his gods, bowed down before them and burned incense to them. *—2 Chronicles 25:14*

Many people have the appearance of religiosity and morality but don't truly believe in God. King Amaziah looked like a believer in the Lord, but he only followed God's commands some of the time. After God gave King Amaziah victory over the Edomites, Amaziah grabbed some of their idols and brought them back to

Judah. Unfortunately, the king didn't put them on a shelf as a souvenir. Amaziah worshiped the gods of the Edomites—the gods who couldn't protect the Edomites from Amaziah's own army and his God. So what accounted for Amaziah's illogical actions? He hadn't committed his whole heart to God (2 Chronicles 25:2). Like King Amaziah, many people have the appearance of piety, but faith in God hasn't penetrated below the surface. They may believe in the Lord when convenience calls for faith, but when persecution or trials come, they turn away. They haven't fully entrusted their lives into God's care.

2 Chronicles 26

King Uzziah was a leper to the day of his death; and he lived in a separate house, being a leper, for he was cut off from the house of the LORD. And Jotham his son was over the king's house judging the people of the land.   —2 Chronicles 26:21

In his early years, King Uzziah trusted God for help, protection, and guidance. But when the Lord gave Uzziah power and wealth, the king depended on these gifts from God rather than on God Himself. Pride swelled and King Uzziah started to consider himself above God's Law. So when the king usurped the role of the priests and burned incense in the temple, God disciplined him. The Lord gave Uzziah leprosy, making him ceremonially unclean. Uzziah's sin resulted in alienation from the community of God until the day he died. Sin and its consequences destroy relationships. Christians today can learn from King Uzziah's example. When we allow pride to direct our thoughts and actions, we risk hurting the people we love and ultimately ourselves as well. Painful wounds caused by pride take a long time to heal.

Therefore, as soon as pride starts to creep into our hearts, we must humble ourselves and seek God's forgiveness.

2 Chronicles 27

So Jotham became mighty because he ordered his ways before the LORD his God. —2 *Chronicles 27:6*

King Jotham made God's Law a priority in his life. He didn't just work the Lord's commands into his life when it was convenient. Jotham organized his thoughts, plans, and motives around God's Law. And because of that, God blessed him. The king built and fortified several cities in Judah, and he defeated the Ammonites and received tribute from them. Today, God doesn't guarantee that Christians will become wealthy and powerful when we obey Him. But we who order our lives around Scripture and allow God's motives to determine ours display spiritual might. Before Jesus Christ's followers had fully comprehended who He was, they recognized that He was "mighty in deed and word in the sight of God and all the people" (Luke 24:19). The Holy Spirit equips believers with the supernatural ability to live our lives according to God's Word. And when that happens, people notice.

2 Chronicles 28

Now in the time of his distress this same King Ahaz became yet more unfaithful to the LORD. —2 *Chronicles 28:22*

With each trial, God gives us an opportunity to trust Him. But with each trial, King Ahaz grew more and more wicked. He burned incense to idols, built altars to foreign deities throughout Judah, and shut the doors of the temple, preventing people from worshiping God. Ahaz even sacrificed his sons to the god Molech. And when the kings of Israel and Aram invaded Judah, Ahaz prayed to idols, not God, for assistance. Never once did Ahaz ask the Lord for help. He just descended deeper and deeper into the abyss of idolatry. When tempests turn our lives upside down, do we cling to the Lord and trust His sovereign care, or do we turn away from Him? Tribulations remind us that we need God. In our suffering, we must cry out to the Lord for help and keep doing what is right according to His Word.

2 Chronicles 29

The priests slaughtered them and purged the altar with their blood to atone for all Israel, for the king ordered the burnt offering and the sin offering for all Israel. —2 Chronicles 29:24

When Hezekiah took over the throne after his father's death, he had a lot of cleaning up to do. King Ahaz had trashed God's temple and caused Judah to forsake the Lord. So King Hezekiah restored temple worship according to the Mosaic Law Hezekiah gathered the priests and Levites and commanded them to consecrate themselves so they could purify the temple and all its furnishings. Finally, the priests placed the offerings on the altar to atone for the peoples' sin. Just as King Hezekiah commanded the priests and Levites to purify God's house and God's people in order to restore proper worship, Christians should examine our lives to see if anything impure resides there. Because Jesus Christ's blood has atoned for our sin once and for all, we don't have to work to compensate for it. But we should regularly ask the Lord to search our hearts, and then we should seek His forgiveness and worship with gladness.

2 Chronicles 30

So they established a decree to circulate a proclamation throughout all Israel from Beersheba even to Dan, that they should come to celebrate the Passover to the LORD God of Israel at Jerusalem. For they had not celebrated it in great numbers as it was prescribed.

—2 Chronicles 30:5

Regularly remembering God's faithfulness and forgiveness is a deterrent against sin. God instituted the tradition of the Passover meal after He led His people out of Egypt so that they wouldn't forget the Lord's miraculous acts on their behalf. God knew that when the Israelites settled in the Promised Land and had abundant food and wealth, they likely would forget Him. And when God's people forget about Him, they often forsake Him. Christians today still need regular reminders of God's grace. The Lord Jesus established Communion as a consistent way to remember God's loyal love and mercy. Just as the Passover recalled Israel's deliverance from Egyptian bondage, Communion recalls our liberation from slavery to sin through Christ. And not only that, Christians now have fellowship with the triune God and with other believers in the community of faith. We must be careful not to neglect or belittle this sacred ordinance.

2 Chronicles 31

Also he commanded the people who lived in Jerusalem to give the portion due to the priests and the Levites, that they might devote themselves to the law of the LORD. *—2 Chronicles 31:4*

God had set aside the priests and Levites to teach the Israelites to observe His Law. They devoted themselves wholly to the work of the temple and to leading God's people in worship, sacrifice, and obedience to God's Law. When God's people obeyed Him, He blessed them with rain, abundant crops, animals, and peace. From the abundance the Lord gave them, He expected His people to meet the needs of the priests and Levites (Numbers 18:8, 21). The Lord still expects the same obedience today. In 1 Timothy 5:18, Paul argued that pastors should receive payment for their labor. The Bible encourages Christians to give generously to our churches so that our pastors can receive an income to support their families. And just like the priests and Levites, pastors must trust God to meet their needs through the provision of His people.

2 Chronicles 32

"With him is only an arm of flesh, but with us is the LORD our God to help us and to fight our battles." And the people relied on the words of Hezekiah king of Judah. —2 Chronicles 32:8

King Hezekiah pointed the people of Judah to the Lord. When faced with the looming threat of the powerful Assyrian army, Hezekiah encouraged God's people and reminded them of the Lord's faithfulness. Even though the king trusted God, he worked hard to protect Jerusalem from Sennacherib, king of Assyria. Hezekiah directed the people to stop up the streams so the land would appear parched and unappealing, and the king's workers built a second wall around the city. But as they fortified the city, King Hezekiah trusted God for protection. Christians, too, can trust that God always fights for His people. When temptation overwhelms, the Lord provides strength. When broken relationships cause pain, God gives comfort. Believers shouldn't turn to secular remedies for problems. Instead, let's turn to the Lord when we face challenges that seem too big to handle; let's watch Him fight for us.

2 Chronicles 33

When he prayed to Him, He was moved by his entreaty and heard his supplication, and brought him again to Jerusalem to his kingdom. Then Manasseh knew that the LORD was God. —2 Chronicles 33:13

No one can out-sin God's grace. When even the worst sinner repents, God is moved with compassion. King Hezekiah's son, Manasseh, came to power at the age of twelve. He eventually abandoned the faith of his father and embraced the idolatry of the surrounding nations. King Manasseh reversed all of Hezekiah's godly reforms. Manasseh rebuilt the high places and encouraged idol worship. He practiced witchcraft and sorcery, used divination, consulted mediums, and burned his sons as sacrifices to an idol. Manasseh seemed beyond hope. But when the Assyrian army captured and tortured him, Manasseh turned to the Lord. And God had mercy. Christians shouldn't consider anyone beyond the grasp of God's grace. The next time we encounter angry atheists or family members who have plunged deep into sin, we should pray. When circumstances bring them to the end of their rebellion, pray that they will repent and turn to the Lord.

2 Chronicles 34

Then they gave it into the hands of the workmen who had the oversight of the house of the LORD, and the workmen who were working in the house of the LORD used it to restore and repair the house.
—*2 Chronicles 34:10*

Josiah became king at the tender age of eight. When he turned sixteen, King Josiah started pursuing a relationship with the Lord. Josiah began removing the high places his father, Manasseh, had built and started restoring God's temple. With all the money the Levites had gathered from God's people, King Josiah hired workers to repair the doors, beams, and furnishings in God's house. These men worked hard, day in and day out, so that God's people could once again worship Him in His temple. These skilled workers played a crucial role in God's redemptive plan. God uses faithful, behind-the-scenes laborers to accomplish His will. As Christians, we shouldn't view public callings as more important than hidden roles. We should seek to honor the Lord in our jobs even when we don't spend our time in the limelight. God is able to use faithful people who do their work to please Him.

2 Chronicles 35

Josiah contributed to the lay people, to all who were present, flocks of lambs and young goats, all for the Passover offerings, numbering 30,000 plus 3,000 bulls; these were from the king's possessions.
—*2 Chronicles 35:7*

Out of his abundance, King Josiah provided for his people. After the workers repaired God's temple, King Josiah reinstituted the Passover meal, which the Israelites hadn't observed while his father, Manasseh, was king. As the people gathered to remember

God's deliverance, King Josiah distributed thirty-three thousand lambs, goats, and bulls among the people so they would have something to offer to God. The Lord had blessed Josiah with wealth, so he shared it with the people. God still expects His people to meet the needs of others. Christians should share what we have with our brothers and sisters in Christ. God places people in our lives who have less than we do so we can learn generosity. And the Lord provides for His people so we can share His gifts with others. When we give of our time, money, and possessions, we learn that all those things belong to God.

2 Chronicles 36

To fulfill the word of the LORD by the mouth of Jeremiah, until the land had enjoyed its sabbaths. All the days of its desolation it kept sabbath until seventy years were complete. —2 Chronicles 36:21

For 490 years, God's land had no rest. It was exhausted and probably not very fruitful—until God forced His people to give the soil in Judah a sabbath. God had commanded His people to work the land for six years but then to let it lie dormant during the seventh year (Leviticus 25:4). But for 490 years, God's people had not kept the sabbath year. He banished them from their land, sending them into Babylonian captivity for seventy years. Finally, the land would have a chance to rest. While the sabbath day and sabbath year no longer apply to Christians, by principle, they still teach us that God expects us to take a break from our jobs and busy routines on a regular basis. As we do so, we demonstrate our trust in the Lord's ability to meet our needs. And with much-needed rest, we will continue to be productive in our work for the Lord.

Ezra

Ezra 1

" 'Whoever there is among you of all His people, may his God be with him! Let him go up to Jerusalem which is in Judah and rebuild the house of the LORD, the God of Israel; He is the God who is in Jerusalem.' "

—Ezra 1:3

When people who don't follow the Lord ascend to positions of power, discouragement often sets in our hearts. *How could God allow ungodly leaders to make decisions that affect our lives?* God's people must have wondered the same thing as they lived as exiles under an endless succession of pagan kings. But even then, God was at work. And when Cyrus, the pagan king of Persia, commanded the Israelite exiles to return to Jerusalem to rebuild God's temple, they knew God had remembered them. Through Isaiah, God had promised to bring His banished people back (Isaiah 45:1–3), and He kept His promise! Believers today don't live in a world where Christians hold every position of power. But we can take courage in this truth: no matter who may rule, God occupies the *highest* throne. The Lord reigns supreme over heaven and earth, and He directs the hearts of kings to achieve His will (Proverbs 21:1).

Ezra 2

Now these are the people of the province who came up out of the captivity of the exiles whom Nebuchadnezzar the king of Babylon had carried away to Babylon, and returned to Jerusalem and Judah, each to his city.

—Ezra 2:1

Ever heard of Seraiah, Bilshan, Mispar, or Bigvai? Most haven't. Before God's people returned to their land, they took a census. They counted every male in every household. All the Israelites dispersed throughout the Persian Empire gathered to make the journey back to Judah. Soon, God's beloved people would be reunited in their land, free to worship Him in His newly rebuilt temple. But first, they had to account for everyone. Often, we skip over chapters in the Bible that list countless unpronounceable names because we think they don't matter. But they do! God wanted to make sure *all* His people made it back from Persia, because He cared about each one. He knows all of His children by name. When we come to chapters like Ezra 2, we should take the time to read each name, remembering God's perfect care for every member of His family—including each of us!

Ezra 3

So they set up the altar on its foundation, for they were terrified because of the peoples of the lands; and they offered burnt offerings on it to the LORD, burnt offerings morning and evening. —Ezra 3:3

When fear swells and anxiety fills our hearts, what do we do first? Hide? Seek out friends and family? Drop to our knees and worship God? When the inhabitants of Judah returned home, they started rebuilding the temple. But before the returned exiles had finished the stone foundation, the Gentiles, who had moved into Jerusalem after God's people left, started hurling stones of insult and intimidation. They didn't want anyone to reintroduce Yahweh-worship and rock the cultural boat. So they threatened God's people. And the Jews, even while shuddering in fear, rebuilt the altar and worshiped God. When we face dreadful situations, where do we turn first? Even in fear, we must worship our Lord, praise Him for His faithfulness, and proclaim our trust in His sovereign protection. God gave His people confidence to follow His will, and He will also help us to obey Him in the face of fear.

Ezra 4

Then work on the house of God in Jerusalem ceased, and it was
stopped until the second year of the reign of Darius king of Persia.
—Ezra 4:24

A new king had ascended the Persian throne—one who had forgotten about Cyrus's decree that freed the Israelites to rebuild the temple. Nevertheless, God's people labored, placing bricks and applying mortar. They had grown used to discouragement from the people of the land. But then the people of the land threatened to halt the Jews' work permanently and wrote a letter to the new king, Artaxerxes, painting God's people as rebels who didn't pay taxes. As a result, Artaxerxes stopped their building project. It didn't resume until the reign of King Darius. Just because roadblocks hinder the work of God's people doesn't mean He disapproves. We can't assume that God is angry with us because we face obstacles. Sometimes God allows us to suffer at the hands of nonbelievers to strengthen our faith and deepen our trust in Him. After all, our spiritual muscles only grow when pressure is applied.

Ezra 5

But the eye of their God was on the elders of the Jews, and they did
not stop them until a report could come to Darius, and then a written
reply be returned concerning it. *—Ezra 5:5*

The Jews had a choice: continue to live in fear or step out in faith. When Haggai and Zechariah visited Jerusalem, they encouraged God's people to resume temple construction. Artaxerxes had halted their building, but God had given them the green light. The law of the land stood against them, but they had the Lord on their side. So they picked up their hammers and trusted God to handle the consequences. When God's people faced persecution for following His commands, God gave them grace to bear it. What was true then is still true. When family members mock us or employers prevent us from sharing our faith or enemies threaten us for claiming Christ, God *will* help us obey Him. Though our actions may result in rejection, intimidation, or death, God's presence will enable us to face it. We need only to ask the Holy Spirit to empower us to live out our faith with confidence.

Ezra 6

They offered for the dedication of this temple of God 100 bulls, 200 rams, 400 lambs, and as a sin offering for all Israel 12 male goats, corresponding to the number of the tribes of Israel. —Ezra 6:17

For one sacrifice, the Jews slaughtered *seven hundred* animals. Doesn't that seem excessive? Couldn't they have put those beasts to a more *practical* use? After much oppression and opposition, the Jews finally finished building the temple. And to prepare it for use according to the Mosaic Law, they held a dedication service. The priests and Levites led the recently returned exiles in a joyful celebration! They held nothing back—they offered their best bulls, rams, and lambs. All seven hundred of them. The word *practical* doesn't contradict our adoration of almighty God. The Lord desires and deserves extravagant, wholehearted worship. He is worthy of our hearts, minds, bodies, time, talents, and treasure! When we hold back, our worship falls short. The Jews rejoiced in the Lord's faithfulness by giving Him their best. We need to follow their example on a daily basis, always taking time to worship God *wholeheartedly* for His grace in our lives.

Ezra 7

*For Ezra had set his heart to study the law of the L*ORD *and to practice it, and to teach His statutes and ordinances in Israel.*

—Ezra 7:10

God's people had moved back to Judah and His temple stood in Jerusalem. Now that His people had a place to worship, God started to rebuild their knowledge of Him. So Ezra the priest—an expert interpreter and teacher of God's Word—went to work. For seventy years, the Jews had lived in exile, in the midst of a godless culture, bombarded with pagan ideas. But once they returned to their land, they had to reestablish the feasts and sacrifices commanded in the Mosaic Law. Ezra, who had committed himself to knowing, obeying, and teaching God's Law, began to instruct God's people. In our day, all too often, we believe we aren't responsible for knowing and teaching God's Word. We leave that to pastors and seminary professors. But God expects *all* Christians to develop an intimate knowledge of His Word. As a kingdom of priests, all believers should understand, obey, and share God's Word with others.

Ezra 8

For I was ashamed to request from the king troops and horsemen to protect us from the enemy on the way, because we had said to the king, "The hand of our God is favorably disposed to all those who seek Him, but His power and His anger are against all those who forsake Him."

—Ezra 8:22

How often do we proclaim our confidence in God and then allow fear to take over? Before Ezra's trip from Persia to Jerusalem, he told the king that God would protect His people from danger on the journey. But as the day of departure drew near, Ezra started to worry. Deep down, Ezra wanted to ask the king for soldiers to accompany them. But since Ezra had already told the king that God would protect them, he kept his mouth shut and, instead, fasted and prayed with his fellow travelers for a safe journey. Even the most godly people, like Ezra, doubt from time to time. Fear, pain, and anxiety are real. God doesn't get angry when our emotions don't match up with what we *know* to be true about Him. His grace covers our fears. The Lord just asks us to pray for His help in our time of need.

Ezra 9

When I heard about this matter, I tore my garment and my robe, and pulled some of the hair from my head and my beard, and sat down appalled. —Ezra 9:3

Tearing one's clothes and yanking out one's hair over a few mixed marriages may seem extreme, but that's exactly what Ezra did! In Deuteronomy 7, Moses prohibited God's people from intermarrying with non-Israelites. Such unions with pagans would lead the Israelites into idolatry. The Lord demanded devotion to Him alone. The mixed marriages in Ezra's day proved that the Jews had not taken God's Word seriously. So Ezra, cut to the heart over the peoples' rebellion, mourned publicly. He feared the Lord and loved His Word, so he begged God to forgive His people. Like Ezra, our reaction to sin reveals what we think about sin. If God's Word isn't a big deal to us, our relaxed response to disobedience will show our true convictions. When was the last time our hearts broke over iniquity in our lives, in our families, or in our nations? What breaks God's heart should break ours too.

Ezra 10

Now while Ezra was praying and making confession, weeping and prostrating himself before the house of God, a very large assembly, men, women and children, gathered to him from Israel; for the people wept bitterly. — Ezra 10:1

How would our lives, our families, or our country change if we approached God's throne with total confidence? If we *really* believed that prayer works? When Ezra prostrated himself before the Lord and asked Him to turn His people back to Him, God answered. After Ezra discovered that some Jews had intermarried with foreigners, he fasted, mourned, and pled for mercy. And as Ezra prayed, the very people involved came to the prophet and confessed. In the middle of Ezra's prayer for grace and guidance, God answered. As Christians, we sometimes doubt that God will answer our prayers like He did for the people of the Bible. But just like God responded to Ezra's plea for mercy, when we cry out for forgiveness, wisdom, or even miracles, our heavenly Father will respond. God may not answer immediately, and He may not always say yes, but we can rest in His attentive care for us as His children.

Nehemiah

Nehemiah 1

"O Lord, I beseech You, may Your ear be attentive to the prayer of Your servant and the prayer of Your servants who delight to revere Your name, and make Your servant successful today and grant him compassion before this man." —Nehemiah 1:11

The wall around Jerusalem lay in ruins . . . and God wanted that wall rebuilt. Nehemiah served as a cupbearer to a Persian king. Hearing of his city's plight, Nehemiah responded not only in action but also in prayer. All of us who follow God's leading must place a high priority on prayer. Prayer makes us wait and forces us to leave the situation with God. Prayer clears our vision because it helps us view the situation through God's eyes. Prayer quiets our hearts because it is God's method for removing our worries. Prayer replaces angst with peace. Knees don't knock when we kneel on them! Prayer activates our faith, because after spending time with the Father, we are more prone to trust Him. God delights in accomplishing what we cannot pull off alone.

Nehemiah 2

Then they said, "Let us arise and build." So they put their hands to the good work. But when Sanballat the Horonite and Tobiah the Ammonite official, and Geshem the Arab heard it, they mocked us and despised us. —Nehemiah 2:18–19

No sooner had Nehemiah received the king's permission to rebuild—no sooner had he urged Jerusalem's Jews to begin the project—opposition arose. Part of the unwritten job requirements for every leader is the ability to handle criticism. That's part of the leadership package. If we never get criticized, chances are we aren't getting anything done. A wise leader will evaluate the opposition in light of its source as well as the spirit and attitude in which the criticism is given. He or she will also consider the voice to which the opposition listens. If our critics listen to God's voice, we had better listen to them. But if they are marching to a different drumbeat, we should use the Nehemiah technique: "Look, they're not even in the same camp. Let's go right on." Because Nehemiah never wandered from God, he was able to handle criticism. The same must be true of us.

Nehemiah 3

Next to them Jedaiah the son of Harumaph made repairs opposite his house. And next to him Hattush the son of Hashabneiah made repairs.   *—Nehemiah 3:10*

Nehemiah had one task, and that was to build the wall around the city of Jerusalem. It doesn't sound very spiritual, but it was God's will for his life. To help complete the task, God led Nehemiah to appoint workmen for various parts of the project. Some were to build certain gates; others, certain sections of the wall. Some were to build in the south; others, north of the city. But everybody had a job to do. This phrase offers a timeless truth that works today as it did then: "Jedaiah . . . made repairs opposite his house." If the wall didn't hold, he had no one to blame but himself. You can bet he did a good job! There's something very motivating about serving in an area that affects us personally. When we serve God, we can often serve Him best in those places we care about the most.

Nehemiah 4

So we built the wall and the whole wall was joined together to half its height, for the people had a mind to work.　　　*—Nehemiah 4:6*

When critics spoke against the Jews' good work, God's people felt demoralized. But Nehemiah urged them to continue—as a result, they made tremendous progress. Intensified opposition against the will of God calls for an intensified response. Nehemiah not only heard the opposition, but he also analyzed available data, prayed, and took decisive, practical action. If we fear that someone might break into our homes, certainly we should trust God. But we should also lock our doors. If we're out of a job, we should pray. But we should also seek opportunities, send out our resumes, and make contacts. It's easier to steer a moving vehicle than one that is stopped. When opposition grows, we should couple prayer with common sense—*and act.*

Nehemiah 5

From the day that I was appointed to be their governor in the land of Judah, from the twentieth year to the thirty-second year of King Artaxerxes, for twelve years, neither I nor my kinsmen have eaten the governor's food allowance.　　　*—Nehemiah 5:14*

Only one challenge proves harder than adversity—and that's advancement. Nehemiah's reaction to his promotion was unhesitating acceptance. Sounds simple, but many Christians are afraid to accept responsibilities that seem beyond themselves. Believers needn't hide in the shadows; we should step up to the plate of opportunity with courage and integrity. When born-again people are promoted to places of leadership, they will have underneath them individuals who rejoice because of their leader's good character. Nehemiah accepted his appointment. Our prayer should be that God would raise up more Christians in strategic spots: college professors, university presidents, business executives, filmmakers, artists, governors, senators, and others who can fashion the minds of the public. There are already some Christians in these roles but not nearly enough.

Nehemiah 6

So the wall was completed. . . . When all our enemies heard of it, and all the nations surrounding us saw it, they lost their confidence; for they recognized that this work had been accomplished with the help of our God. —*Nehemiah 6:15–16*

"The wall was completed." Only four words, but what a magnificent accomplishment! With the completion of the wall, the tables of intimidation turned. Nehemiah's enemies lost their confidence. That had to be the most thrilling experience in the world— for the people to see God come to the rescue when they had been helpless. In the middle of the incessant assault of the enemy, in spite of the endless verbal barrage, the wall was erected! Even as the enemy blasted, God built. We need this reminder today because it is impossible to do the will of God, to walk by faith, to build those walls without suffering attack by the enemy. Persistence pays rich dividends. If honor is at stake, if a good principle is at stake, if we know we're accomplishing something that would please the Lord, we should never, *never* quit.

Nehemiah 7

Now the city was large and spacious, but the people in it were few and the houses were not built. Then my God put it into my heart to assemble the nobles, the officials and the people to be enrolled by genealogies. —Nehemiah 7:4–5

Nehemiah 7 provides a description of Jerusalem's administrative structure and shows how the city became well organized, well defended, and well governed. The wall reconstruction project was finally complete. But the city still lacked something—people. This illustrates a timeless truth: it is pointless to have a well-constructed superstructure if little or no life exists on the inside. This is not only true in the family of God; the same can be said of any organization. We've all experienced the steely, impersonal touch of institutional efficiency. People are not manufactured cogs that can be processed by non-thinking machines. We are highly individual, complex creatures, with motives and needs. We require strong, sensitive leadership, not isolation. Nehemiah's census called together various classes of people and helped get them organized. Getting people united, protected, and relating smoothly with one another remains vitally important.

Nehemiah 8

Then on the second day the heads of fathers' households of all the people, the priests and the Levites were gathered to Ezra the scribe that they might gain insight into the words of the law. —Nehemiah 8:13

For a full day prior, the people of Jerusalem had listened as Ezra read the Scriptures. They absorbed the facts, but they still lacked true insight. Several factors will always be necessary to gain spiritual understanding. First, it takes time. The people had to process what they learned before they came back to build upon that foundation. Second, it takes the right people. The people specifically sought out Ezra the scribe to teach them the Scriptures. The Bible repeatedly affirms the importance of godly people imparting life's wisdom to those willing to learn it. That's the third factor: it takes a teachable attitude. The older leaders were members of Ezra's peer group, and yet they said, "Teach us." They demonstrated a genuine desire to learn. Sometimes the Lord wants to deliver the insight we need through our peers. But if we are to learn from them, we must come with a teachable attitude.

Nehemiah 9

"Do not let all the hardship seem insignificant before You,
Which has come upon us, our kings, our princes, our priests, our
*   prophets, our fathers and on all Your people,*
From the days of the kings of Assyria to this day."   Nehemiah 9:32

This section of the longest prayer in the Bible is particularly authentic in its pain and humility. When the suffering we endure as a consequence of our own sin bears down, it's natural to wonder how much the Lord cares about our pain. If it's a result of our own sin, we deserve to hurt, don't we? So why *should* He care? Like most of us in our weaker moments, the Jews projected their own fleshly attitudes onto God. How easy to forget God's mercy, God's grace. We need to pray honestly and express how we feel (even if it isn't theologically astute). We should dare to pray what we authentically think and feel. If we're doubtful of His love for us, we should tell Him! If we're angry with Him, our heart should express it and confess it. He already knows everything about us. He won't be shocked. We aren't hiding anything from Him.

Nehemiah 10

All those who had knowledge and understanding, are joining with their kinsmen, their nobles, and are taking on themselves a curse and an oath to walk in God's law . . . and to keep and to observe all the commandments of God our Lord, and His ordinances and His statutes. —*Nehemiah 10:28–29*

The document that God's people wrote and signed drove a literary stake into the ground, erecting a written monument that established their purpose and values. Making verbal promises is fine, but as fallen creatures who are given to weakness and second-guessing, it helps if we document our decisions. Serious thought precedes any significant change, but written plans confirm right priorities. If we really want to achieve our primary goals, we should write them down and refer to them often. Complex, ethereal thoughts become straightforward, concrete strategies when spoken or put in ink. Our thoughts may be good, but they will remain forever entangled if they haven't been thought through and written down. The ability to put first things first will elude us until our purpose, objectives, and plans are written out.

Nehemiah 11

Now these are the heads of the provinces who lived in Jerusalem, but in the cities of Judah each lived on his own property in their cities — the Israelites, the priests, the Levites, the temple servants and the descendants of Solomon's servants. —Nehemiah 11:3

Nehemiah 11 lists five specific groups who gave to the work of the Lord — even though their giving remained anonymous. These included those who willingly moved into the city, those who willingly worked within the temple, those who were in charge of the outside work of the house of God, those who prayed, and those who sang for the services of the house of God. In God's eyes, no contribution is ever insignificant. Our gifts and abilities make us valuable, although not necessarily famous. What's more, the Lord remembers every labor done in love (Hebrews 6:10). Our rewards from God will be based on faithfulness, not on applause. The public may never know the ministries we do in the shadows. But God never checks with them to measure the merit of our service or to determine our rewards. The willing unknowns are not unknown to God.

Nehemiah 12

On that day they offered great sacrifices and rejoiced because God had given them great joy, even the women and children rejoiced, so that the joy of Jerusalem was heard from afar. —Nehemiah 12:43

At the dedication of Jerusalem's completed wall, the Jews rejoiced over God's provision. They sang together, and their joy flooded the hillside so all could hear and be glad. Had their circumstances changed? No, *the people* had changed. One great application pours out of these verses: happiness is not dependent on outward circumstances but upon inward choices. When we choose to focus on what's truly important in any situation, we can smile and sing through an experience and come out rejoicing. It all depends on what—or who—we make our focus. Few things are more magnetic than a smile or a cheerful disposition, especially among those in God's work. The people under Nehemiah's leadership felt the freedom to be joyful. Let's give those we serve alongside that same freedom.

Nehemiah 13

Remember me, O my God, for good.   *—Nehemiah 13:31*

After Nehemiah's leave of absence from Jerusalem to attend to his Persian duties, he returned to the holy city to discover major problems. Despite the fact that the resident Jews had made a commitment to remain faithful to God, they had compromised in the areas of maintaining financial integrity, obeying the Sabbath, and preserving domestic priorities. Nehemiah refused to be passive; he took the problems by the throat. But he also modeled the timeless truth that courageous conviction must be tempered with deep devotion. This is where many well-meaning Christians miss it. It is significant that the final verse in Nehemiah's book shows him on his knees in prayer. He had fought hard for the right, but he had kept his heart soft before the Lord. What a magnificent model he was! He was a man of honesty, conviction, and devotion. We should follow his example.

Esther

Esther 1

On the seventh day, when the heart of the king was merry with wine, he commanded . . . the seven eunuchs who served in the presence of King Ahasuerus, to bring Queen Vashti before the king with her royal crown in order to display her beauty to the people and the princes, for she was beautiful. But Queen Vashti refused to come.
—Esther 1:10–12

Put bluntly, the king was drunk. In this inebriated state, he decided to show off another of his prizes: the physical beauty of his queen. He ordered her to be brought into the banquet hall, wearing her royal crown. He wanted his own private beauty pageant for all of his drunken guests to enjoy . . . and envy. The queen, however, just said no! In the midst of an unsavory scene, Vashti was brave enough to say no to that which was blatantly wrong. In resisting this insulting act of indignity, she took a stand against the greatest power in her universe. Submission does not mean that a wife is a sexual pawn to fulfill the carnal desires of her husband. It was never God's design that a wife submit to her husband's evil desires. Marriage does not give a husband the right or the license to fulfill his basest fantasies by using his wife as a sex object.

Esther 2

The king loved Esther more than all the women, and she found favor and kindness with him more than all the virgins, so that he set the royal crown on her head and made her queen instead of Vashti.
—Esther 2:17

God's people are not excluded from high places because they have known handicap or hardship. Esther was a Jew exiled in a foreign land. She was an orphan. She was light-years removed from Persian nobility. Yet none of that kept God from exalting her to the position where He wanted her. Regardless of our level of faith or our rank in society, most Christians experience times when we discount the significance of our days. We find ourselves sighing rather than singing. We wonder what good can come from all the bad around us. We have kids we can't handle and marriages that lack harmony. We live with pressures that seem to have no purpose. Whether we see Him or not, God is at work in our lives at this very moment. He specializes in turning the mundane into the meaningful. God not only moves in unusual ways, He also moves on uneventful days. He is just as involved in the mundane events as He is in the miraculous.

Esther 3

After these events King Ahasuerus promoted Haman, the son of Hammedatha the Agagite, and advanced him and established his authority over all the princes who were with him. —Esther 3:1

Mordecai had uncovered the plot to kill the king and had told Esther, who then had told the king. Mordecai was the one who had saved the king's life. So why did Haman get the promotion? Because life is not only painful; it is also unfair. We start telling ourselves, "I will be promoted because I have worked the hardest, I have come up with the big ideas, I am the one who's done the most for my boss; therefore, it's only right that I be given that special position I have been anticipating." Well . . . we should be prepared, because it probably won't happen. This isn't an attempt at pessimism. This is reality. Wrong happens! Life isn't fair. Why? Because of evil. When righteousness rules, justice reigns. But when evil lurks in a heart, injustice follows. That's what happened when Haman, of all people, was given authority and promoted.

Esther 4

In each and every province where the command and decree of the king came, there was great mourning among the Jews, with fasting, weeping and wailing; and many lay on sackcloth and ashes.

—Esther 4:3

Haman had ordered the annihilation of all the Jews throughout the 127 provinces of the Persian kingdom. He had the extermination plan put into writing, and he sealed it with the king's ring. The order left the general public bewildered and confused. When the king's command went out from Susa and into the provinces, the people fell into widespread sorrow and loud mourning. Though we do not court it, suffering pushes us out of our homes. It puts us in touch with our neighbors. Natural disasters, violence, and severe illness touch us all at some point. Hardships like these force us to grab hands with one another and pull closer together. Suffering never ruined a nation! Hardship doesn't usually fracture families. Affluence does! But not suffering. It reduces everybody to the same level with the same goal: survival.

Esther 5

Esther said, "If it pleases the king, may the king and Haman come this day to the banquet that I have prepared for him." —Esther 5:4

Esther had learned of Haman's plot to annihilate all the Jews. Now, standing before the king, she had her moment to bring down the roof on top of Haman—but she didn't. Not yet. This wise woman understood the value of timing. She wasn't in a hurry, nor was she revengeful. She was waiting on the Lord. When we wait on the Lord, we don't sit in a corner contemplating infinity or walk around in a daze humming "Sweet Hour of Prayer." We don't have to go out on a hillside, eat birdseed, and strum a guitar. We don't have to go barefoot, wear a robe, and live in a hut in Tibet for the winter. Sometimes, of course, we need to sit quietly, by ourselves, alone with the Lord for a time of quietness. Solitude and silence are wonderful when nourishing our souls. But mostly, while we are waiting on God, we go right on with our business.

Esther 6

During that night the king could not sleep so he gave an order to bring the book of records, the chronicles, and they were read before the king. It was found written what Mordecai had reported concerning Bigthana and Teresh, two of the king's eunuchs who were doorkeepers, that they had sought to lay hands on King Ahasuerus.
—Esther 6:1–2

Mordecai had made a courageous decision when he exposed the evil plot to kill the king. But no one ever rewarded Mordecai for his great act. It seemed as though no one noticed or remembered. So, up until this sleepless night in Susa, Mordecai had gone on living his life unnoticed, unrewarded, and unappreciated. This situation is nothing new today, but it can still put us in a tough spot. Perhaps a decision or discovery of ours caused someone else to be promoted to a place of significance, and now that person has all the glory, the status, the salary, and the celebrity, while we've never even been recognized, to say nothing of thanked or rewarded. Believers today can learn a lesson from Mordecai: never stoop to becoming a person of vengeance. We must guard our hearts against it, just as Mordecai did, patiently avoiding opportunities to get even or to speak against the one who has wronged us.

Esther 7

So they hanged Haman on the gallows which he had prepared for Mordecai, and the king's anger subsided.   —Esther 7:10

Though the king eventually punished Haman by executing him, Esther and Mordecai had to wait for God to act in their favor through the king. The waiting must have been excruciating. Their story reminds us that the workings of God are not related to our clocks; they are related to our crises. God's timing is unrelated to planet earth's clock time. So while waiting on God, believers can look beyond the present. The best way to do that is to *pray*! We tell God, in anguish if necessary, the horror of the waiting. We express our panic. We tell Him we're trapped. It's okay for us to ask Him to hurry up, if that helps. (He can handle it!) Sometimes we don't know how we can stay afloat much longer. In those moments, we turn to Him to help us see beyond the pain of the present. Prayer offers inner support when meaning is absent or unclear.

Esther 8

In each and every province and in each and every city, wherever the king's commandment and his decree arrived, there was gladness and joy for the Jews, a feast and a holiday. And many among the peoples of the land became Jews, for the dread of the Jews had fallen on them.
—Esther 8:17

With Haman out of the way, the king decreed that the Jews would live and could protect themselves from any hostile force. What amazing relief Esther must have felt, following her husband's new edict! Imagine the gladness and joy that swept across the city of Susa—in every face, "in each and every province and in each in every city" (Esther 8:17)—once the news started spreading! We're talking one massive, in-the-street celebration for all the Jews, with singing and music and dancing and laughter and wall-to-wall joy! In our spiritual lives, when those old walls of stubbornness, fear, and gloom are torn down, what's better to do than celebrate? And talk about infectious! The gladness of our hearts, the joy on our faces, the overall, unrestrained fun among us attracts others to our Lord. It always will. People cannot stay away from the audacious, attractive joy of God's people!

Esther 9

Then said Esther, "If it pleases the king, let tomorrow also be granted to the Jews who are in Susa to do according to the edict of today; and let Haman's ten sons be hanged on the gallows." So the king commanded that it should be done so; and an edict was issued in Susa, and Haman's ten sons were hanged.   *—Esther 9:13–14*

Esther had the respect of her husband. When she made a suggestion, he gave it the careful consideration it deserved, since it came from his own wife. Some women today don't have the respect and trust from their husbands that Esther had from hers. And from that perspective, Esther's story is almost too perfect. Many women today have lingering pain. Some have pretty horrendous heartaches. Some have memories they wish they could erase. No matter how hard they try, those scenes just won't go away. As a result, some wives try new strategies. They hold back their love and affection. They fight fire with fire. They pout and whine and write harsh letters. They have affairs. But despite the pain, God's people cannot pay back evil for evil (Romans 12:17). The only true solution to retaliation and revenge, the only way to get past blame and resentment, and the only antidote for secret, smoldering feelings of rage from the pain of the past is forgiveness.

Esther 10

For Mordecai the Jew was second only to King Ahasuerus, and great among the Jews and in favor with his many kinsmen, one who sought the good of his people and one who spoke for the welfare of his whole nation. —*Esther 10:3*

Mordecai had risen to the highest position in the land, save the king himself. There isn't anything in Mordecai's background or in the surrounding Persian culture to suggest that one of God's people, the Jews, would have any hope of occupying such a prominent place in the government. But God is full of surprises. That's why He chose a harlot to help the spies (Joshua 2:1–4). That's why He chose a rebellious prophet to lead the Greater Nineveh Evangelistic Crusade (Jonah 1:1–2). And that's why He lifted a no-name from the gate of the king and made him a prime minister. God delights in lifting up nobodies and turning them into somebodies. As Paul wrote to the Corinthians, "not many mighty, not many noble" (1 Corinthians 1:26)—in other words, not many blue bloods—are called. God has chosen the despised and many of the losers of the world to turn their lives around and follow the One who died on a cross.

How to Begin a Relationship with God

Many people consider the Old Testament irrelevant—filled with archaic phrases, places, and people. But God still speaks powerfully through the Old Testament to change lives. Through the good news found in His Word, the Lord breathes eternal life into sick souls. From Genesis to Revelation, God reveals four essential truths we all must accept and apply if we are to find the life-transforming remedy for our sick souls. Let's look at these four truths in detail.

Our Spiritual Condition: Totally Depraved

The first truth is rather personal. One look in the mirror of Scripture, and our human condition becomes painfully clear:

> "There is none righteous, not even one;
> There is none who understands,
> There is none who seeks for God;
> All have turned aside, together they have
> become useless;
> There is none who does good,
> There is not even one." (Romans 3:10–12)

We are all sinners through and through— totally depraved. Now, that doesn't mean we've committed every atrocity known to humankind. We're not as *bad* as we can be, just as *bad off* as we can be. Sin colors all our thoughts, motives, words, and actions.

If you've been around a while, you likely already believe it. Look around. Everything around us bears the smudge marks of our sinful nature. Despite our best efforts to create a perfect world, crime statistics continue to soar, divorce rates keep climbing, and families keep crumbling.

Something has gone terribly wrong in our society and in ourselves—something deadly. Contrary to how the world would repackage it, "me-first" living doesn't equal rugged individuality and freedom; it equals death. As Paul said in his letter to the Romans, "The wages of sin is death" (Romans 6:23)—our spiritual and physical death that comes from God's righteous judgment of our sin, along with all of the emotional and practical effects of this separation that we experience on a daily basis. This brings us to the second marker: God's character.

God's Character: Infinitely Holy

How can God judge us for a sinful state we were born into? Our total depravity is only half the answer. The other half is God's infinite holiness.

The fact that we know things are not as they should be points us to a standard of goodness beyond ourselves. Our sense of injustice in life on this side of eternity implies a perfect standard of justice beyond our reality. That standard and source is God Himself. And God's standard of holiness contrasts starkly with our sinful condition.

Scripture says that "God is Light, and in Him there is no darkness at all" (1 John 1:5). God is absolutely holy—which creates a problem for us. If He is so pure, how can we who are so impure relate to Him?

Perhaps we could try being better people, try to tilt the balance in favor of our good deeds, or seek out methods for self-improvement. Throughout history, people have attempted to live up to God's standard by keeping the Ten Commandments or living by their own code of ethics. Unfortunately, no one can come close to satisfying the demands of God's law. Romans 3:20 says, "By the works of the Law no flesh will be justified in His sight; for through the Law comes the knowledge of sin."

Our Need: A Substitute

So here we are, sinners by nature and sinners by choice, trying to pull ourselves up by our own bootstraps to attain a relationship with our holy Creator. But every time we try, we fall flat on our faces. We can't live a good enough life to make up for our sin, because God's standard isn't "good enough" — it's *perfection*. And we can't make amends for the offense our sin has created without dying for it.

Who can get us out of this mess?

If someone could live perfectly, honoring God's law, and would bear sin's death penalty for us — in our place — then we would be saved from our predicament. But is there such a person? Thankfully, yes!

Meet your substitute — *Jesus Christ*. He is the One who took death's place for you!

> [God] made [Jesus Christ] who knew no sin to be sin on our behalf, so that we might become the righteousness of God in Him. (2 Corinthians 5:21)

God's Provision: A Savior

God rescued us by sending His Son, Jesus, to die on the cross for our sins (1 John 4:9–10). Jesus was fully human and fully divine (John 1:1, 18), a truth that ensures His understanding of our weaknesses, His power to forgive, and His ability to bridge the gap between God and us (Romans 5:6–11). In short, we are "justified as a gift by His grace through the redemption which is in Christ Jesus" (Romans 3:24). Two words in this verse bear further explanation: *justified* and *redemption*.

Justification is God's act of mercy, in which He declares righteous the believing sinners while we are still in our sinning state. Justification doesn't mean that God *makes* us righteous, so that we never sin again, rather that He *declares* us righteous—much like a judge pardons a guilty criminal. Because Jesus took our sin upon Himself and suffered our judgment on the cross, God forgives our debt and proclaims us PARDONED.

Redemption is Christ's act of paying the complete price to release us from sin's bondage. God sent His Son to bear His wrath for all of our sins—past, present, and future (Romans 3:24–26; 2 Corinthians 5:21). In humble obedience, Christ willingly endured the shame of the cross for our sake (Mark 10:45; Romans 5:6–8; Philippians 2:8). Christ's death satisfied God's righteous demands. He no longer holds our sins against us, because His own Son paid the penalty for them. We are freed from the slave market of sin, never to be enslaved again!

Placing Your Faith in Christ

These four truths describe how God has provided a way to Himself through Jesus Christ. Because the price has been paid in full by God, we must respond to His free gift of eternal life in total faith and confidence in Him to save us. We must step forward into the relationship with God that He has prepared for us — not by doing good works or by being a good person, but by coming to Him just as we are and accepting His justification and redemption by faith.

> For by grace you have been saved through faith;
> and that not of yourselves, it is the gift of God;
> not as a result of works, so that no one may
> boast. (Ephesians 2:8–9)

We accept God's gift of salvation simply by placing our faith in Christ alone for the forgiveness of our sins. Would you like to enter a relationship with your Creator by trusting in Christ as your Savior? If so, here's a simple prayer you can use to express your faith:

> *Dear God,*
>
> *I know that my sin has put a barrier between You and me. Thank You for sending Your Son, Jesus, to die in my place. I trust in Jesus alone to forgive my sins, and I accept His gift of eternal life. I ask Jesus to be my personal Savior and the Lord of my life. Thank You. In Jesus's name, amen.*

If you've prayed this prayer or one like it and you wish to find out more about knowing God and His plan for you in the Bible, contact us at Insight for Living. Our contact information is on the following pages.

We Are Here for You

If you desire to find out more about knowing God and His plan for you in the Bible, contact us. Insight for Living Ministries provides staff pastors who are available for free written correspondence or phone consultation. These seminary-trained and seasoned counselors have years of experience and are well-qualified guides for your spiritual journey.

Please feel welcome to contact your regional Pastoral Ministries by using the information below:

United States

Insight for Living
Biblical Counseling Department
Post Office Box 269000
Plano, Texas 75026-9000
USA
972-473-5097, Monday through Friday,
8:00 a.m. – 5:00 p.m. central time
www.insight.org/contactapastor

Canada

Insight for Living Canada
Biblical Counseling Department
PO Box 8 Stn A
Abbotsford BC V2T 6Z4
CANADA
1-800-663-7639
info@insightforliving.ca

Australia, New Zealand, and South Pacific

Insight for Living Australia
Pastoral Care
Post Office Box 443
Boronia, VIC 3155
AUSTRALIA
1300 467 444

United Kingdom and Europe

Insight for Living United Kingdom
Pastoral Care
PO Box 553
Dorking
RH4 9EU
UNITED KINGDOM
0800 787 9364
+44 (0)1306 640156
pastoralcare@insightforliving.org.uk

Resources for Probing Further

God doesn't just want Christians to increase their knowledge about Him and His Word. Our heavenly Father wants His children to know Him more intimately and apply His Word to our lives. Shelves and shelves of books exist that tell us what the Bible says, but finding resources to help us *apply* its principles to everyday life is a bit more challenging. So we have compiled a list of resources that won't just take up space on your bookcase—they will help you live out God's Word each day. Keep in mind as you read these books that we can't always endorse everything a writer or ministry says, so we encourage you to approach these and all other non-biblical resources with wisdom and discernment.

Insight for Living. *Insight's Bible Application Guide: Genesis–Deuteronomy — A Life Lesson from Every Chapter*. Plano, Tex.: IFL Publishing House, 2012.

Insight for Living. *Insight's Old Testament Handbook*. Plano, Tex.: IFL Publishing House, 2009.

Merrill, Eugene H. *Everlasting Dominion: A Theology of the Old Testament*. Nashville: Broadman & Holman, 2006.

Merrill, Eugene H. *Kingdom of Priests: A History of Old Testament Israel*. 2nd ed. Grand Rapids: Baker Academic, 2008.

Morgan, G. Campbell. *Life Applications from Every Chapter in the Bible*. Grand Rapids: Fleming H. Revell, 1994.

Swindoll, Charles R. *David: A Man of Passion and Destiny*. Great Lives Series. Nashville: Thomas Nelson, 2008.

Swindoll, Charles R. *Elijah: A Man of Heroism and Humility*. Great Lives Series. Nashville: Thomas Nelson, 2008.

Swindoll, Charles R. *Esther: A Woman of Strength and Dignity*. Great Lives Series. Nashville: Thomas Nelson, 2008.

Swindoll, Charles R. *Fascinating Stories of Forgotten Lives: Rediscovering Some Old Testament Characters*. Great Lives Series. Nashville: Thomas Nelson, 2011.

Swindoll, Charles R. *Hand Me Another Brick: Timeless Lessons on Leadership*. Rev. Ed. Nashville: Thomas Nelson, 2007.

Wiersbe, Warren W. *The Wiersbe Bible Commentary: Old Testament*. Colorado Springs: David C. Cook, 2007.

Wiersbe, Warren W. *With the Word: The Chapter-by-Chapter Handbook*. Nashville: Thomas Nelson, 1991.

Ordering Information

If you would like to order additional copies of *Insight's Bible Application Guide: Joshua – Esther* or order other Insight for Living Ministries resources, please contact the office that serves you.

United States

Insight for Living
Post Office Box 269000
Plano, Texas 75026-9000
USA
1-800-772-8888, Monday through Friday,
7:00 a.m.–7:00 p.m. central time
www.insight.org
www.insightworld.org

Canada

Insight for Living Canada
PO Box 8 Stn A
Abbotsford BC V2T 6Z4
CANADA
1-800-663-7639
www.insightforliving.ca

Australia, New Zealand, and South Pacific

Insight for Living Australia
Post Office Box 443
Boronia, VIC 3155
AUSTRALIA
1300 467 444
www.insight.asn.au

United Kingdom and Europe

Insight for Living United Kingdom
PO Box 553
Dorking
RH4 9EU
UNITED KINGDOM
0800 787 9364
www.insightforliving.org.uk

Other International Locations

International constituents may contact the U.S. office through our Web site (www.insightworld.org), mail queries, or by calling +1-972-473-5136.